Louis
ARMSTRONG
and His Concert Group

The Program

Due to the ad lib quality of this music no formal program is possible. It is likely, however, that the following numbers will be heard.

Indiana
High Society
Cornet Chop Suey
Dear Old Southland
Monday Date
Big Butter and Egg Man
Struttin' With Some Barbecue
That's For Me
Pennies From Heaven
St. Louis Blues
Ain't Misbehavin'
Rockin' Chair
Rose Room
St. James Infirmary Blues

Wiffenpoof Song
Confessin
Royal Garden Blues
Back O'Town Blues
I Can't Give You Anything But Love
Mop Mop
Save It Pretty Mama
Muskrat Ramble
At the Jazz Band Ball
Blueberry Hill
Some Day .... a new ballad written by Mr. Armstrong
Basin Street Blues .... a duet
Sugar

WITHDRAWN

elma Middleton Vocalist.
PROVED
REEL
Free
SCOTC
Magne
Satchmo at the Crescendo
SIDE NO. 1
PATENT
APPLIED
FOR
A. by MINNESOTA MINING AND
3M COMPANY
MANU
sota

For Phoebe

In association with the

Louis Armstrong Archives

and Foundation

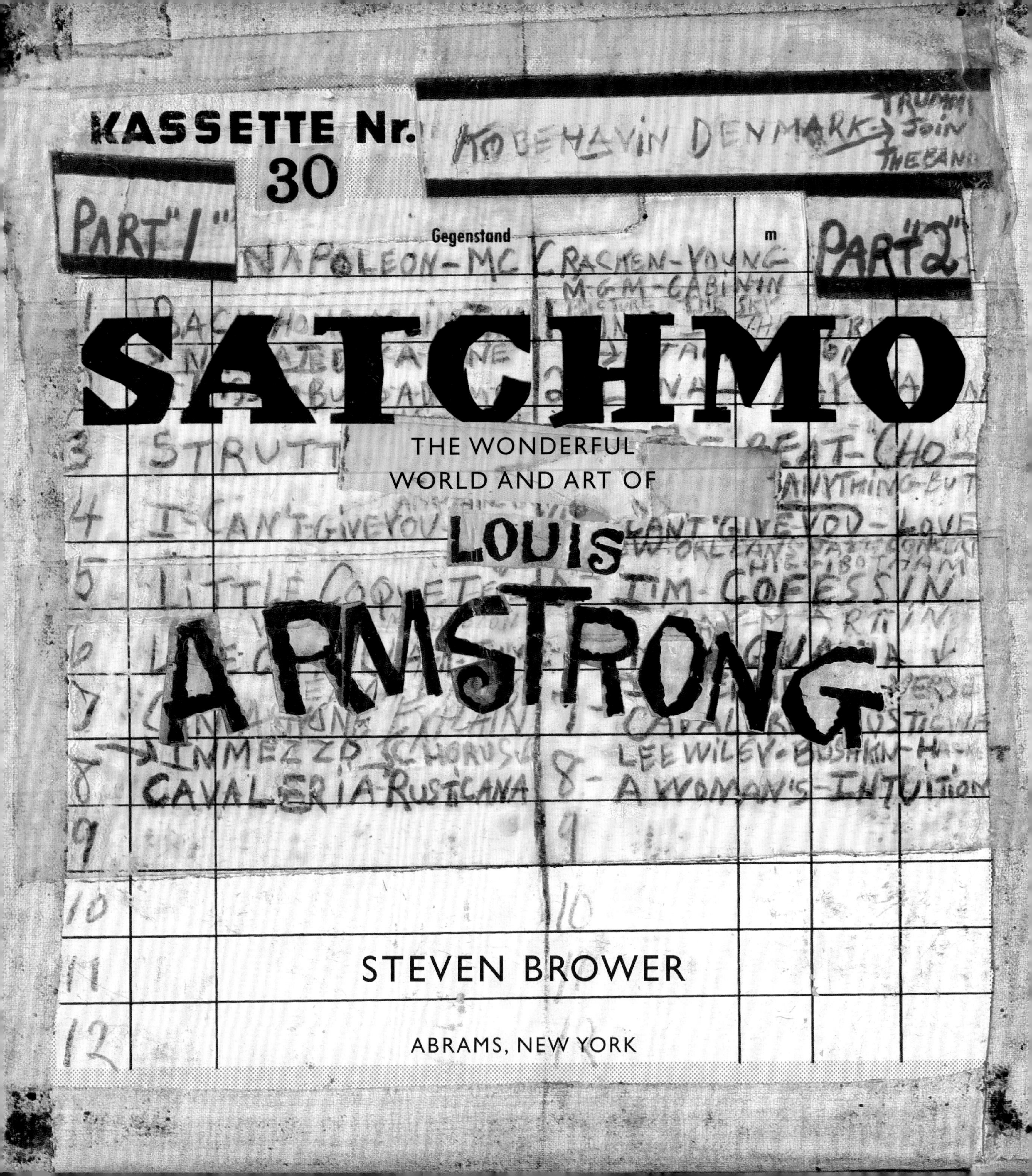

SATCHMO

THE WONDERFUL WORLD AND ART OF

LOUIS ARMSTRONG

STEVEN BROWER

ABRAMS, NEW YORK

Contents

Foreword

WONDERFUL TOWN

You know how it is, you want to look and you don't want to look—especially when it comes to the transmogrification of blackness into showbiz.

In the 1920s, when Harlem became another satellite in America's entertainment constellation, white patrons with an eye for dusky talent hot-footed it up to the Cotton Club and Connie's Inn. There, starting in the late 1920s, they began to hear the work of a New Orleans, Louisiana–born trumpet player, singer, and artist named Louis Armstrong, who played in Fletcher Henderson's band, then the most prominent "Negro" band in the city.

In Harlem, Satchmo, as Armstrong was affectionately called, developed a voice that could alternate with his horn. The voice Billie Holiday said inspired her own; a voice that was like a fine, deep drawing etched against the tinfoil-shimmery, artificial crooning of the time. Take for instance his 1931 recording of "Lazy River," which was one of the bestselling records of the year. On the acetate, his voice becomes the lazy river; it unfurls like a muddy thought. In "Lazy River," Harlem-born natives may have heard what they were descended from: Southern-born slaves—Armstrong's grandparents were slaves—who hardly wanted any truck with what James Baldwin called "the old country."

But America was all their country. Armstrong just described it, with that voice, and using that instrument, which could crack and soar like his smile. Later, he revealed that the source of his smile wasn't a need to please white people. Indeed, he admitted that he smoked pot every day because there were white people in America—less a skin color than a political stratagem, one centered on the exploitation of privilege. That makes an American, too: knowing how deeply other Americans can hate you. He also wore a Star of David around his neck, having been clothed and fed as a child by Jewish immigrants in New Orleans. In a sense, he was equal parts understanding: of being despised, and of being loved by those who were despised.

Even though it was not in Harlem but in Queens where Armstrong eventually settled with his beloved fourth wife, Lucille, the artist never really lived anywhere: He was a performer. He lived in dressing rooms and hotel rooms, waiting to go on, slightly stoned, appearing to be happy. Happiness for him was another mask, like the makeup he wore, occasionally, to get through this show or the next. Evidence of his rather complicated relationship to being seen can be found here in *Satchmo: The Wonderful World and Art of Louis Armstrong*, the first extensive collection of his collages. Hundreds of collages, which are still housed in Queens, amount to a self-portrait of sorts, albeit a fractured one. Composed between 1953 and 1971, these images are of Armstrong's "body . . . and a future with this body," according to Franz Kafka, another artist who understood something about life in the margins. In Armstrong's collages, we see the artist with Lucille, but underneath a hailstorm of scribbles, bits and pieces of paper, tape, as though the image of his rich and complicated love for her couldn't be contained in a photograph. Another image: of Armstrong playing his horns, his hands separated from his face, concentrating, lips pursed, everything forgotten except the music.

Or had he forgotten it? The bad managers and death threats? The hatred of blacks who, by the 1960s, thought his "Lazy River" jazz was old school and bad news? Collage, like drawing, is, as the poet Marianne Moore had it in another context, "a radiograph of the soul." These images reveal Armstrong's soul to have been writerly in its density. They became a visual autobiography made from his pen and paper and scissors to cut up the way he saw the world, and to represent—accurately—how Americans are cut up but insist on being put back together again, with dreams.

—*Hilton Als*

The tape-box collages, scrapbooks, photographs, manuscripts, and other materials presented in this book are provided by the Louis Armstrong House Museum, Queens College. The website of the Louis Armstrong House Museum is www.louisarmstronghouse.org.

TIMELINE

1906

Born August 4, in New Orleans, Louisiana. Raised by grandmother, Josephine.

Attends Fisk School for Boys.

Goes to live with mother, Mayann.

1901

1907

**1910–
1920**

Sells newspapers on streets, works
collecting scrap metal for the Kornafsky
family, begins playing tin horn, delivers
milk for Cloverdale Dairy, sings on
street corners in group.

1912

Arrested for firing a gun on
New Year's Eve, sent to Colored
Waifs' Home, joins Waifs'
Home Band, run by Capt. Jones,
coached by Peter Davis.

Phonograph recordings
supersede sheet music
in sales throughout the
United States.

**1908–
1912**

Drops out of Fisk School in
the middle of fifth grade.

1913

Introduction

There's that note. It comes at the end of "In My Solitude" and in "Yours and Mine," as well as "Got a Bran' New Suit." The many others have been well documented. The clarion opening fire shots of "West End Blues," the jaunty swing of "I've Got Rhythm and Jubilee." This one's different. It is the plaintive cry from the soul of the experienced. It is a yearning call, striving, reaching, faltering, then succeeding. It is the voice of a life well lived, one that understood all too well the struggles inherent, and never surrendered. If this note still exists, cascading across the universe as pure sound wave, and is received by beings on other planets, it will stand as testament of life on planet earth during the twentieth century.

Goes to live with father and stepmother; returns home with mother; begins playing cornet in bands.

1915

Plays with Fate Marable's band on the steamship *Streckfus Steamers*; marries first wife, Daisy Parker.

1919

Delivers coal.

1914

1918

Replaces Joe "King" Oliver in Kid Ory's Band; leaves New Orleans to play on steamships out of St. Louis with Marable's band.

And who is it that created these sounds? He is frequently cited alongside Mickey Mouse and Charlie Chaplin as the most recognizable of twentieth-century American icons. A personality so large he simply could not be known by one name. He answered to Little Louis, Dip, Dippermouth, Gate, Gatemouth, Rhythm Jaws, Satchelmouth, Satchmo, Ambassador Satch, or Pops, a salutation of respect he bestowed on others as well, but he was Louis to those who knew him, and Louie to those who didn't. Billie Holiday called him "the Landlord" because "he owns the building."[1]

No description defines him: He was at once a singer, musician, songwriter, entertainer, performer, actor, movie star, celebrity, writer, ambassador of goodwill, and as it turns out, a talented and dedicated collagist. He helped to blur the distinctions between high and low art, rendering them meaningless. He is credited with not only facilitating the redefinition of our American musical heritage but our very culture as well. He is even attributed with coining the following words in our hip vernacular: cats, chops, crazy, daddy, face, gate, gutbucket, jive, mellow, pops, scat, solid.

He had a sound so large that he was forced to stand twenty feet behind the rest of the band during single microphone recording sessions, so as not to overpower them. His charisma could overshadow and

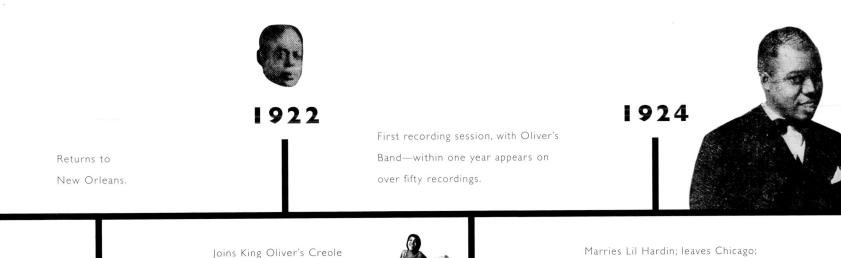

1922

First recording session, with Oliver's Band—within one year appears on over fifty recordings.

1924

Returns to New Orleans.

Joins King Oliver's Creole Jazz Band in Chicago.

Marries Lil Hardin; leaves Chicago; joins Fletcher Henderson's band in New York; backs up Ma Rainey, Bessie Smith, and others.

1921

1923

outshine all the others with whom he performed, if he so chose. When he began to play his cornet, audiences would scream.

Even his birth date is in dispute, although he steadfastly hung on to the more romantic of the two, July 4, 1900.

Songs he wrote and cowrote are so much a part of American heritage that many seem to have no author at all: "I Wish I Could Shimmy Like My Sister Kate," "Hear Me Talking To Ya," "Someday (You'll Be Sorry)," as well as scores of others. He popularized such traditional standards as "When the Saints Go Marching In" and he was the only

performer to make the song charts and *Billboard* list every decade from the 1920s until the 1960s, when his version of "Hello, Dolly!" knocked the Beatles off the charts in 1964. Armstrong then again hit the charts in the 1980s when his song "What A Wonderful World" appeared on the sound track of *Good Morning, Vietnam* seventeen years after his death.

Louis Armstrong is largely regarded as the single most important, creative, and influential figure in jazz history. He is erroneously credited with the creation of jazz, as well as the invention of scat singing, although he was present at the 78 rpm inception of jazz, exuding a profound influence over its

1926–1928

1925

"Muskrat Ramble," recorded with the Hot Five, is a top-ten hit.

Moves back to Chicago; joins the Dreamland Syncopators with Lil; first recording with his own band, the Hot Five.

1926

Records with Earl Hines and Erskine Tate; plays hundreds of session dates, including those with Bessie Smith and Ma Rainey.

development, and recorded one of the first instances of the later.

His improvisation and tour-de-force playing set the standard for all who followed. Many agree that Armstrong taught America and the world how to sing. As Bing Crosby noted, "Do you realize that the greatest pop singer in the world that ever was or ever will be forever and ever is Louis Armstrong?"[2] He grimaced and twisted his lower lip to produce vocalizations as if he were playing an instrument. He spoke and sang in a gravelly everyman husk, masking a beautiful tenor. He was an alchemist, transforming everything he touched. His covers of pop songs swung. He even imbued racist minstrel songs with a sense of virility and defiance—he lifted up anything he touched with authority and confidence.

He appeared in over thirty films and dozens of television spots. His autobiographical writing is at once honest, profound, colorful, and engaging, written in a singular, warm voice, although by his own admission his education did not extend much beyond the fifth grade. As actress Tallulah Bankhead understood: "He uses words like he strings notes together—artistically and vividly."[3]

Typing was his second favorite thing to do after music. Out of his typewriter he poured pages upon pages of autobiographical sketches and letters to friends, in

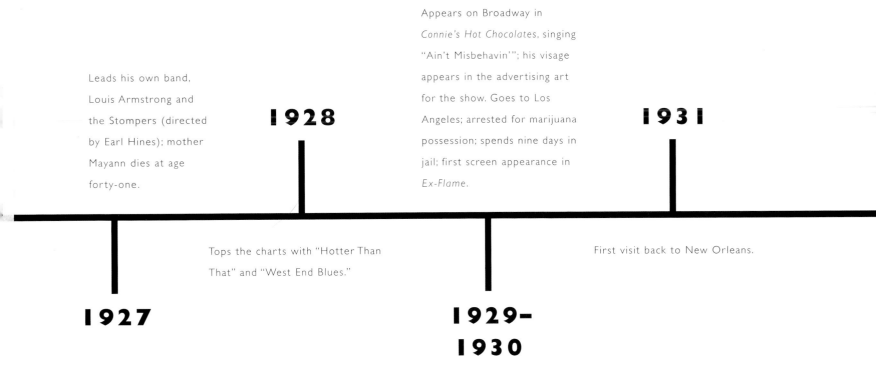

Leads his own band, Louis Armstrong and the Stompers (directed by Earl Hines); mother Mayann dies at age forty-one.

1928

Appears on Broadway in *Connie's Hot Chocolates*, singing "Ain't Misbehavin'"; his visage appears in the advertising art for the show. Goes to Los Angeles; arrested for marijuana possession; spends nine days in jail; first screen appearance in *Ex-Flame*.

1931

Tops the charts with "Hotter Than That" and "West End Blues."

First visit back to New Orleans.

1927

1929–1930

distinctive green ribbon. He preferred the same color when writing in longhand, telling stories, jokes, off-color and "on."

He was often surrounded by controversy, despite the fact that he continually denied being political. His bands were among the very first to be integrated, and he often broke color barriers as they toured. He was one of the first African Americans to be sponsored on the radio and his All-Stars were the highest paid jazz band of their era. He believed in the healing power of music to cross all barriers, political or social: "A note's a note in any language."

He was married four times and had numerous paramours. He was also a lifelong proponent of marijuana use.

He was a person of tremendous generosity who strongly believed in respect for all, and viewed his art as a gift dedicated to "the cause of happiness." When he had the brick facade of his home in Corona, Queens, redone, he treated all his neighbors on the entire block to the same, so as not to appear above the rest. His wit, unpretentiousness, unpredictability, warmth were the stuff of legends. He gave away money in the thousands to friends, fans, those in need.

But what of his relationship to the visual arts? Other than the work itself, there is little commentary in

1932

Returns to London; tours Europe; tours Scandinavia; greeted at train station in Copenhagen, Denmark, by ten thousand fans; lip bursts, forcing him to take off four months; first of many texts, a letter, is published by the English review *Melody Maker*; has top-ten hit with "Hobo, You Can't Ride This Train."

1934

Returns to U.S. and to Chicago; Joe Glaser becomes manager; fronts Luis Russell's band; has double-sided top-ten hits with "I'm in the Mood for Love" and "You Are My Lucky Star."

First European tour aboard the SS *Majestic*; greeted by journalist Percy Brooks as "Satchmo," an English corruption of Satchelmouth, which quickly becomes his personal favorite and best-known alias; opens at the London Palladium; has top-ten hits with "Sweethearts on Parade" and "Body and Soul."

1933

Plays Paris: "I had to take so many bows until I wound up taking 'em in my bathrobe."

1935

Armstrong's own writings about why he felt compelled to spend so much time creating collages. We do know that he would spend hours talking into a reel-to-reel tape recorder on the road, and while at home in a working-class neighborhood of Corona, Queens, reminiscing about his astonishing career. He would then adorn the tape boxes with collages culled from newspaper clippings, movie stills, ads, greeting cards, photographs, as well as his own hand lettering. In addition, he created scrapbooks of his own experiences, which also serve as a highly personal record of African American history from segregation through the civil rights movement.

Early on others saw the relationship between Armstrong's sonic stream of consciousness and other art forms. Tristan Tzara, poet, essayist, and one of the founders of the Dada movement, wrote of Armstrong's talent: "Louis Armstrong is a poet whose efforts of expressing himself in words are frustrated with each successive trial, because in the final analysis, poetry cannot be put into words. In his personal language, however, this poetry touches the sensitivity of individuals from all four corners of the world."[4]

Perhaps the answer lies in the fact that Armstrong himself was represented in others' artwork, as early as the 1920s. Arnold Genthe, a photographer known for his depictions

1936

Appears in the film *Artists and Models* with Martha Raye; has top-ten hit with "Public Melody Number One."

Appears in the film *Pennies From Heaven* with Bing Crosby.

1937

Receives Academy Award nomination for his performance in the film *Going Places*; divorces Lil Hardin; marries Alpha Smith.

1938

Appears in *Swingin' the Dream* on Broadway; has top-ten hit with "When the Saints Go Marching In."

1939

of San Francisco's Chinatown and the 1906 San Francisco earthquake, was one of the first to record the early New Orleans jazz scene in the 1920s, but due to the racism of the times, no African Americans were included. Soon afterward, however, artists such as Jules Pascin, a Bulgarian painter, depicted the same scene, including people of color.[5] Simultaneously others began to represent the emerging jazz scene in New York, including American artists such as Charles Demuth, Reginald Marsh, Archibald Motley, Jr., German émigré Winold Reiss, French painter (and jazz promoter) Charles Delaunay,

Mexican painter and caricaturist Miguel Covarrubias. Shortly afterward Armstrong himself would be depicted in both paintings and newspaper illustrations, and as befitted his celebrity, his visual doppelgänger would continue throughout his lifetime. Well-known illustrators and cartoonists Al Hirschfeld and E. Simms Campbell would soon render his visage, and he even made appearances in animated cartoons in the early thirties. Ben Shahn would illustrate his biography for film and print, and painters such as Stuart Davis and Arthur Dove would use Armstrong's music as a source of inspiration. Davis described this influence thusly: "Every artist has models of greatness in the arts which

1942

Lucille buys a home; on tour three-hundred-plus dates per year.

1946

Forms the All-Stars; plays Carnegie Hall and Town Hall in New York City.

Marries Lucille Wilson, a Cotton Club dancer.

Returns to New Orleans; has top-ten hit with "You Won't Be Satisfied (Until You Break My Heart)," a duet with Ella Fitzgerald.

1943

1947

guide his development. Louis Armstrong has always been one of the most important for me. Not to illustrate his musical ideas, but as an example of direct expression which transforms its Subject Matter into Art."[6] African American collagist Romare Bearden, himself a musician, would often include Armstrong in his work.

Armstrong's own collages predate Bearden's, starting perhaps as early as the 1930s and in force throughout the fifties and sixties. There are over twenty scrapbooks and 650 tapes in existence, more often than not adorned with energetic collages. Most utilize photographs he had collected over the course of his lifetime, some utilize greetings cards and telegraphs of

good cheer that he received from presidents and royalty, and others are of more artistic flights of fancy. Others still are risqué, employing lingerie ads and revealing photography. Whether Armstrong was inspired by the art around him, and indeed art about him, is unclear. It is understood that his education was limited at best, and it is doubtful he had much exposure to the visual arts as a child.

Still, the relationship between jazz improvisation and collage is clear. Armstrong himself referred to his music as "rag time" rather than "jazz," the term "rag" referring to the "ragging" of tunes by plantation workers; that is, to take an existing melody, such as the European songs the plantation owners would play, and improvise

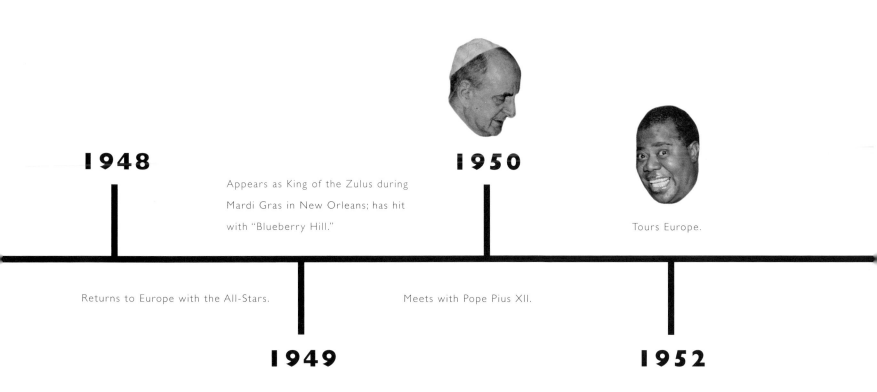

1948

Appears as King of the Zulus during Mardi Gras in New Orleans; has hit with "Blueberry Hill."

1950

Tours Europe.

Returns to Europe with the All-Stars.

Meets with Pope Pius XII.

1949

1952

on top of and around the melody, to create something new. Armstrong's collages work in the very same manner: he is taking an existing work, cutting it up, rearranging it, creating something fresh—a visual ragging, if you will.

Perhaps the roots of Armstrong's collages (like his music) do not lie with the world of media and art but deeper in his origins. African American folklorist and author Zora Neale Hurston, writing in the early part of the twentieth century, noted, "The need to adorn is the second most notable characteristic in Negro expression. . . . It arises out of the same impulse as the wearing of jewelry or the making of sculpture—the urge to adorn. On the walls of the homes of the average Negro one finds a glut of gaudy calendars. Wall pockets and advertising lithos . . . I saw in Mobile a room in which... the walls were gaily papered with Sunday supplements of the *Mobile Register*. There were seven calendars and three wall pockets. . . . The mantel-shelf was covered with a scarf of deep homemade lace, looped up with a huge bow of pink crepe paper. Over the door was a huge lithograph showing the treaty of Versailles . . . decorating a decoration . . . did not seem out of place to the hostess. . . . The feeling back of such an act is that there can never be enough beauty, let alone too much. . . . Whatever the Negro does of his own volition he embellishes."[7]

Another possible early influence on the

1955 Performs at a benefit concert at the Royal Festival Hall in London for Hungarian refugees, accompanied by the Royal Philharmonic Orchestra; duets with Ella.

1959 Tours internationally: Africa, Australia, Czechoslovakia, Formosa (Taiwan), France, East and West Germany, Great Britain, Hong Kong, Hungary, Iceland, India, Japan, Korea, Mexico, the Netherlands, New Zealand, Romania, Singapore, Scandinavia, and Yugoslavia.

Satch Plays Fats, a tribute to Fats Waller, is a top-ten LP.

Returns with the All-Stars to Europe; becomes seriously ill in Italy.

1956

1960s

impressionable young Armstrong was the parades in his native New Orleans, where the participants dressed in festive colors, homemade masks and costumes, and were joined by musicians as they marched. The profound effect of the music has been d_____ g's visual re_____ You want to_____ y Bechet.[8] _____ joyed the er_____ dering his vo_____ over onto th_____ to ceiling, at_____ em down.

He would also give away collages as gifts. Conversely he would solicit friends to send him photographs and adverstising placards featuring him and his band for him to use.

Perhaps Louis describes his raison d'être best. In a letter to Marili Marden dated September 27, 1953, he wrote ". . . My hobby is to pick-out different things during what ever I read and piece them together and make a little story of my own . . . of course it's not an awful lot to send a person . . . but somethimes [sic], the spirit of the thing can mean so much. . . ."

One thing is certain: Armstrong believed in the healing power of his music and, by extension his art,

1961

Has number-one hit with "Hello, Dolly!," knocking the Beatles off the top of the charts; wins Grammy for best vocal performance.

1968

Performs at the Newport Jazz Festival, (singing only, on doctor's orders) to thunderous applause.

All-Star Velma Middleton dies on tour in Sierra Leone; records with Duke Ellington.

1964

Records *Disney Songs the Satchmo Way*, introducing him to an even younger generation; "What a Wonderful World" becomes a number-one hit in the United Kingdom.

1970

July 6, 1971, dies of heart failure; more than twenty-five thousand people view his coffin.

to cross all barriers, political, social, high and low, "in the cause of happiness." Ambassador Louis. As Tallulah Bankhead wrote in *Flair* magazine on the occasion of his fiftieth birthday, ". . . artists certainly arise from time to time who are supreme but, except for unique genius, most of us require conditioning in a social or cultural context to appreciate particular kinds of art, whereas in the case of the transcendent genius, a meaning implicit in the artistic product comes through which makes it meaningful to everyone above and beyond the confines of one's limited cultural back yard."[9]

"The bottom line . . ." Tony Bennett noted, "is what did we contribute to the world? We contributed Louis Armstrong." Or as trumpeter Lester Bowie said, "He revolutionized the aspect of music as an art form, and as a musician being a cultural leader. . . . His influence is undeniable, it's unmistakable and it's eternal."[10]

So come, cats, dig Louis Armstrong, his art, his generosity, his life lived large, his writing, him. In the final analysis, it is the spirit of the thing that can mean so much. When all is said and done, it is a wonderful world. And in the end, there's that note.

—*Steven Brower*

The Early Years,
1901–1921

Red Beans and Rice

**I'm just the same as one of those
people out there in the audience.**

—*Louis Armstrong*[11]

It is the stuff legends are made of. Louis Armstrong, the twentieth century's most important and influential musician and singer, star of stage and screen, was the man who topped the music charts in every decade, from the 1920s till the 1960s. "Satchmo," as we have come to affectionately adore him—luminous performer, stellar writer, and yes, talented collagist. He was an artist of great import and significance who overcame abject poverty and hardship to become one of the most democratic of stars to employ the most democratic of art forms—collage.

There is some irony that the birth date he chose for himself, or rather the one he steadfastly hung on to, would be the same as "The Father of American Music" from the prior century, Stephen Foster, born July 4, 1826, and famous initially for writing minstrel songs. For Louis David Armstrong, born either July 4, 1900, or August 4, 1901—whichever you prefer—the grandson of slaves, would become the next century's "Father of American Music," helping to transform a regional musical style into a popular art form and along the way overcoming the racist society that Foster helped glamorize.

Armstrong was a revolutionary, and as such had more than his share of controversy along the way.

He shared his fanciful birthday with another purveyor of American music, George M. Cohan, who also wasn't truly born on July Fourth:

I was a Southern Doodle Dandy born on the Fourth of July, 1900. My mother Mary Ann—we called her Mayann—was living in a two-room shack in James Alley, in the Back O' Town colored section of New Orleans. It was in a tough block, all them hustlers and their pimps and gamblers with their knives, between Gravier and Perdido Streets.

—*Louis Armstrong*[12]

"Little Louis," the first of many monikers to come, was born and raised near the very un-story-book-like section of New Orleans known as Storyville. But nobody tells his own story better than Louis, and he blessed us with several renditions: his wonderful *My Life in New Orleans*, published in 1954, and many autobiographical sketches, lovingly typed for magazine editors, friends, and fans alike.

It is a testament to Armstrong's generosity and goodwill, which would become distinct aspects of his personality in adulthood, that he recalled these days so

so here goes:From the day l was born in James Alley,some say Jane but
to me it is just plain ol James Alley.It was on the Fourth of July a
blasting 4th of July,1900,my mother calls it when l came into the world
and they named me the fire cracker baby.................

James Alley was the toughest short street or neighborhood ever heard
of.It was a little street running from Gravier to Perdido about one half
block and from White to Broad streets,actually it was about one good
block long. My mother said the very day l came into the world there
was a big killing.A character who was known as the badest guy in the
Alley killed another fellow,his name was Red Cornelius,May-ann said
when Red got tired of cutting you he would take out his gun and shoot
you a little..........................

This small but compact neighborhood had everything in it that made up
fast living(sporting type) people.Prostitutes,pimps,gamblers,pick -
pockets and most everything imaginable.The thing that has amazed me to
this day was the respect all of these people had for the little Church
that was located in the the block....................

My Grandmother raised me after my mother had to go out to do days wash-
ings in the white folks yard in order for us to eat.My father was a
pretty sharp,tall and handsome cat,he was the Grand Marshall of the
Odd Fellows Lodge,naturally the gals wouldn't let him get along with
his family.

Mary-ann and my father Willie Armstrong were separated for two years
then they desided to go back together at which time my sister Beatrice
(mama Lucy) was born. That makes me two years older than my sister.

Speaking of the first time l began to listen to good music especially
good Cornet playing was at the Funky Butt Hall right accross the street
from Fisk School.They gave a dance every saturday night but before the
band could go on the stand they had to play for one half hour out in
front of Funky Butt Hall before they got the job.This was called playing
on the Banket (side walk).While they played out there we would stand on
the other side and listen to the music.Thats when l heard Buddy Bolden
play that fine cornet.He was really a great guy and the Strongets on
that horn.When they finished on the Banket they would go inside and
play until four in the morning.

The next great player l heard were Joe Oliver.Bunk Johnson,Buddy Petit
along with Buddy Bolden.As the years passed and l grew up around Funky
Butt,Joe Oliver and Bunk Johnson won out as top cornet men,because the
really great Buddy Bolden would cut hair all day in his barber shop,
play music over half of the night and dicipate the rest of the night
so it finially got the best of him.He went insane from blowing the horn
too hard.l have never heard any more from that great musician.From then
on it was Joe Oliver and Bunk Johnson upmost in my mind.

The Funky Butt gave me quite a bit of my ear for music and inspiration.
They would play Ragtime,Fox trots,Waltzs,Tangos,Mazookas,Schottische in
fact all kind of tempos which helped me through the years to play with
different orchestras,symphany,show music etc. ....

fondly. The South in general, New Orleans in specific, was entrenched in segregation. As a dark-skinned black, Louis was limited as to where he could go, both within the city and in life. Yet as many other African Americans did in the South, he discovered music as a liberating force.

...arisma, Louis's first musi... ...n street corners and play... ...strument constructed out o... ...s strung across it. He purcl... ...elp of the Karnofskys, a Jew... ...or whom he collected scrap metal. Music was everywhere, flowing from the doors of bars, and parades commemorating the

COLORED WAIFS' (JONES') HOME
1913 NEW ORLEANS, LOUISIANA 1913

departed and holidays. Celebrations continued to play an important part in his early life. On New Year's Eve in 1913, he was arrested for the first time:

Very few arrest of minors were made Tuesday . . . the most serious case was that of Louis Armstrong, a twelve year old negro, who discharged a revolver at Rampart and Perdido Streets. Being an old

offender he was sent to the Negro Waifs' Home.
—The Times Democrat, January 2, 1913.[13]

Once he entered the Colored Waifs' Home, he was instructed by music teacher Peter Davis, whose strict discipline provided structure, and he emerged from the home a cornet player, modeling himself on existing greats Bunk Johnson, Buddy Petit, Buddy Bolden, and his hero Joe Oliver. He would spend the rest of his life paying tribute to "King" Oliver, and even portrayed his mentor on the television show You Are There in 1954.

Soon he was playing in many of the marching bands throughout the city, on holidays and at funerals.

Yeah, Pops—jazz actually rose from the dead . . . the real music came from the grave. That was how jazz began. That is why it brings people to life. —Louis Armstrong[14]

Mature well beyond his years, Louis first married at age sixteen. Soon after, Louis's teenage cousin Flora Hatfield asked him on her deathbed to adopt her son Clarence, a promise Armstrong kept throughout his life, although no legal papers were filed. Sadly, Clarence was injured falling off a balcony as a toddler and was mentally disabled as a result.

Louis's precociousness eventually led to his replacing his idol Oliver in Kid Ory's band. Despite his assuming so many adult responsibilities at such a young age, Louis managed to retain a mischievous desire to explore the new and be awed by the wonder of the world around him—attributes he was able to sustain throughout his life. As someone who by his own account did not benefit from more than a fifth-grade education,

Below: Little Louis with his mother Mayann and little sister Mama Lucy (Beatrice) in 1920 in New Orleans. **Next page:** In his second published autobiography, Louis omitted any mention of the Karnofsky family, the Russian Jews who immigrated to New Orleans, which is surprising considering the profound influence they played in his early life. By employing him to collect scrap metal with their son, they provided him the money to purchase his first horn at age eight, and in the evenings he participated in singing with the family. For the rest of his life, Louis wore a Star of David they gave him as a present. While hospitalized in 1969, Louis decided to set the record straight. In this passage he also discusses a visit to a Chinese restaurant with his mother and sister, reveling in New Orleans diversity, albeit not integration.

Reel "68" 33/4

In the 1940's — and particularly after the last war ... was a rather self-conscious movement to return to the roots of jazz and to smaller, more intim... t for Armstrong there was no need seek the origins, for he was, virtually, jazz.

The only change was that his playing becam... . With his All-Stars to-day he is more relaxed and smoother than in the past, ... nt as ever, with that superb tonal sense. He can always keep the tempo alive ... y tempo other than his seems wrong.

He is probably the only trumpeter of ... s technique and his strength. He will almost certainly keep on playing until his grea... y look good for plenty yet. He conserves his energy to-day like an ageing but still great br... you hear him, that fine, hopeful tone could be no one else's.

Louis Armstrong, his sister Beatrice and its mother sit for a formal picture in 1920. Louis was playing at The Orchard Cabaret in New Orleans arning $21.00 a week. He was composing tunes like "I Wish I Could Shimmy Like My Sister Kate."

1

Of course the Jewish Folk Folks had a better break than the Negroes. Because they are white people. That's what was so Puzzling to me. Just the same they had hard times for a long time. THE KARNOFFSKYS PAPA + MAMA CAME FROM RUSSIA — BEFORE I WAS BORN —

The Chinese finaly Moved into a little section of their own, and Called it China Town. with a few little beat up RESTAURANTS. Serving Soul Food on the same Menu of their CHINESE dishes. I used hear the Negroes bragging about their Lead Beans and Rice. Thats the way a CHINESE Waiter would order it for you. Lead Beans + Rice. was int bad at all. Of course the Colored people Cook the best Red Beans and Rice. But for a Change And something different, My mother and My step Father used to take me + Mama Lucy (My Sister) down in China Town + have a Chinese Meal for a Change. a kind of Special Occasion. And the Bill in those days were real cheap. And we felt as though we were having something Big. We would also order Fried Rice and Livers Gravy. with our Red Beans. And ooh God — you would lick your fingers' it would taste so good.

his literary achievements are as remarkable as his musical ones. And as is the case with young rebellious spirits, there were those who would try to censor and repress his exuberant essence, and try their best to box him in.

His improvised, groundbreaking solos brought about a shift in music, altering it forevermore from melodic collective playing, tightly arranged, to that of a solo player rising above the rest. His irrepressible personality came through loud and clear.

On the riverboats Armstrong learned to read music, and he was heard by a wide range of audiences and musicians up and down the Mississippi, including white horn players Bix Beiderbecke and Jack Teagarden. He became equally well known for his unique singing style and onstage patter.

In the small hours, a friend and I were wandering around the French quarter, when suddenly I heard a trumpet in the distance. I couldn't see anything but an excursion boat gliding through the mist back to port. Then the tune became more distinct. The boat was still far off. But in the bow I could see a Negro standing in the wind, holding a trumpet high and sending out the most brilliant notes I had ever heard. It was jazz. It was what I had been hoping to hear all through the night. I don't even know whether it was "Tiger Rag" or "Panama." But it was Louis Armstrong descending from the sky like a god. The ship hugged the bank as if it were driven there by the powerful trumpet beats. I stayed absolutely still, just listening, until the boat dropped anchor.—*All-Stars trombone man Jack Teagarden, remembering his 1921 New Orleans visit*[15]

Following this time on the ship, Louis's mentor Joe Oliver, now dubbed "King," sent for Louis to join him in Chicago. In 1922, Armstrong made the pilgrimage to join Oliver's Creole Jazz Band. It is there that Louis's musical genius is captured on record for the first time, playing on Oliver's session dated April 5, 1923. Shortly thereafter Armstrong recorded the very first sessions with his own band, the Hot Five, featuring his new paramour, pianist Lil Hardin.

Armstrong's playing on these recordings is nothing short of visionary. His solos portray varied tones and shifting viewpoints, poetry in motion, rapid-fire repartee, displaying an adventurousness that is idiosyncratic and unique, so many shifts and cuts, as though he were viewing the melodies from all angles, like a Cubist collage. Through chiaroscuro-like shading and sheer exuberance, he transformed everything he touched and made it his own.[16]

Indeed, a publicist in an early advertisement dubbed Armstrong the "Master of Modernism."[17] The embracement of modernity that came at the century's turn was reaching a crescendo in the 1920s. Modern art, such as Cubism, Dadaism, and Futurism—combined with Streamline to give it a look, and Armstrong was at the forefront, giving it a voice. Thereafter, the twenties roared and the Jazz Age was born.

Yet there was nothing at all elite about the man. His approach to music, to art, and to life was to share, to cast himself as an everyman for the masses. On the

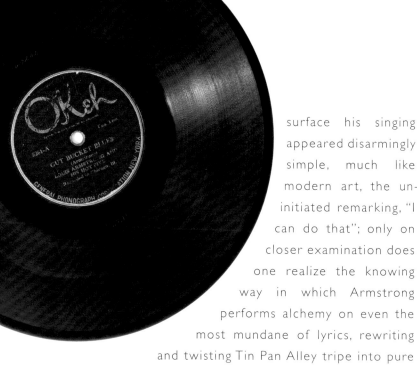

surface his singing appeared disarmingly simple, much like modern art, the un-initiated remarking, "I can do that"; only on closer examination does one realize the knowing way in which Armstrong performs alchemy on even the most mundane of lyrics, rewriting and twisting Tin Pan Alley tripe into pure gold, just like Picasso turned newspaper, metal, and wood assemblage into art.

Singing was more into my blood than trumpet. —*Louis Armstrong.*[18]

His voice was an instrument all unto itself, unique. He moved his mouth and body to produce different sounds, contorting his features to hit and shape notes. He imbued everything he touched with the force of his personality. He never allowed the lyrics to stand in the way of his improvising and having a good time. In fact this led to one of the first recordings of "scat" singing during the session for "Heebie Jeebies." In what is most likely an apocryphal tale, the story goes that the lyrics sheet fell off the music stand, causing Louis to begin to sing nonsense lyrics.

Eef, gaff, mmmff, dee-bo, duh-deedle-labahm . . . Rip-bip-ee-doo-doot, doo . . . —*Louis Armstrong*

This tale is akin to that of Wassily Kandinsky entering his painting studio to discover an easel upside down on the floor—thus discovering abstract

art. In reality, scat lyrics had been used by comedians to the delight of audiences throughout the South. It was Louis's genius to wed it to jazz, freeing singers from restrictive lyrics forever, and placing them in the center of creativity along with the band.[19] Armstrong's first record under his own name, *Heebie Jeebies*, was a tremendous triumph, selling forty thousand copies in three weeks at a time when a total sale of ten thousand was deemed a success.[20]

Another performing technique Louis brought with him from New Orleans, and one that would provide controversy throughout life, was mugging, that is, widely grinning and using body language for a laugh. Armstrong, a natural comedian, had no greater desire than to bring joy to his audience. In addition he would parody ministers, of whom he was critical, delivering mock sermons to the audiences' and his own amusement.[21] Still, mugging had its roots in minstrelsy, and as time went on this became one of the most controversial and contested aspects of Louis's oversized personality. He, however, remained unabashedly unrepentant throughout his career.[22]

What is forgotten by many people is that throughout his career Armstrong did more to further the cause of racial equality than any other African American performer of his generation. He was the best-known American black celebrity in the late 1920s, and was the first to integrate his bands. He was the first to receive equal billing to white movie stars in Hollywood feature films and the first African American to

Page 128

The Armstrong Story

She didn't take time to send me a wire or nothing,she just got the very first train that she could get and started for Chicago.

One night just before the show got started,1 looked up a nd to my surprise there was my mother coming across the stage, bundles,bags and all.She had spied me and no one on earth could stop her,she had seen her boy and that was all it was to it.She ran like mad into my arms to greet me. Everybody turned around to look at us.My dear mother didn't care what the world had to say,all she was interested in was her little sloe-footed boy,(that was me),I was speechless.

When my mother reached me,across the Band Stand,I hadn't closed my mouth and it had been opened every since I spied her.I was so very happy,I didn't know actually what was going on until she said,"How is my boy.How are you doing?" I realized my mother was actually there before me,in Person.Everything was real great.Oh! my sucha hugging and kissing. Every body in the band got around my mother inclu\ding King Oliver.The first intermission all of us gathered around her. There wasn't anything to do but sit and listen to her talk,May-Ann told us all the news from home after she found out 1 was o.k. That was when she told us a- bout some cat coming down to New Orleans and telling everybody she had better go to Chicago at once and see about her boy,(me of course).May-ann asked the fellow why her son didn't come home? That cat told my mother ,he had asked me the same question.He said" Louis just held his head down and cried." Dig that cat. I told mama,"Can't you just imagine me tuning up this face of mine and crying." That gag put my mother in very good spirit,she laughed out aloud.The rest of the night she had lots of fun meeting the cats in the band.........1

When the Lincoln Gardens show was over,we played a short dance set then we were off for the rest of the night.I rented a room for the night for my mother,until I could get her an apartment for her.While we were on our way home 1 asked my mother how she liked the big city?.She said in a sad voice,"Son I don't think 1 like up north with all of these new fangled gaget,(meaning) all the modern things they had in Chicago,which they didn't have in New Orleans.New fangled gaget, was May-Ann's pet phrase.It was used to express New Inventions,etc..............

Joe Oliver was a glad to see my mother as 1 was.... Oh! she was very proud of her son......She beamed all over every time she looked at me.When the show was over at the Gardens Papa Joe and I took May-Ann to Thirty-Fifth and State streets,to the Arlington Restaurant and had a real good Southern cooked breakfast ....

Speaking of the good old times,we really had one with my mother her first time in Chicago.She was in good spirit by the time we had finished our breakfast and talked about all the happenings around New Orleans after we had left.We nearly talked her to death.Each of us had different people we wanted to know how they were doing where they had gone.There were so many I wanted to know about,all of my old WHITE BOYS childhood pals the ones I played cowboy and Indians with in our good old school days...WE..WERE...THE...INDIANS

After we had scarfed,"we decided to call it a day and go home.We needed a good EATEN night sleep. May-Ann needed to go in too so we cut out.I was so happy when I got her straightened out,I knew she was tired but she wanted to be sure I was fine. Some how I wanted her to like chicago now that she was in town..........

O.K.
I HAD'NT SEEN HER IN SUCH A LONG TIME - UNTIL I JUST COULDINT TAKE MY EYES OFF HER.

host a nationally syndicated radio show. He transformed Fats Waller's "Black and Blue" from the lament of a dark-skinned jilted lover, by eliminating lyrics, to a protest song of the first order. He possessed the uncanny ability to alternate between the comic and the serious from song to song.[23]

He managed to imbue racist minstrel songs like "Shine" (about the plight of a shoeshine boy) or "When It's Sleepy Time Down South" ("Hear those banjos ringing, the people are singing / They dance till the break of day, hey") with such authority that he overcame the material, both on record and on film. Thus, he challenged our very notions of high art and low, of self-expression versus mass appeal. Yet he remains one the twentieth century's most misunderstood figures.

Look at the nice taste we leave. It's bound to mean something. That's what music is for. —*Louis Armstrong*

LOUIS ARMSTRONG
And His Orchestra

ROCKWELL - O'KEEFE INC., RADIO CITY

1920s

Hear Me Talkin' To Ya

Armstrong lived well in Chicago, in his own apartment with his own private bath and toilet, which was not bad for a kid who grew up in a two-room apartment with an outhouse. It was during these early years that he purchased a typewriter and began writing letters home. With a musician's ear for language, he expressed himself with lively, playful, yet clear words strung together like a horn solo.[24] He invented his own style of punctuation, using ellipsis not to indicate missing words but rather in the way a musician indicates a pause.[25]

Over time his literary oeuvre numbered in the thousands of pages and included two published autobiographies and a censored third, numerous memoirs, magazine articles, book reviews, and letters, typed or written out in longhand on yellow pads, created backstage, often with others frequently present multitasking in today's parlance—or in hotel rooms during his endless touring. He could write dozens of pages in a single sitting.[26] No other jazz musician, and perhaps major star of his time and stature, left behind such a great outpouring of the written word.[26]

Of course I am not so bad myself at "Swimming."—In fact it's one of my "famous" Hobbies, outside of typing—I loves that also.

—Louis Armstrong[27]

Later on in life, once he became less transitory and bought a home, he turned to collage, which no doubt was a close third.

Armstrong left Oliver's band in 1924 and traveled to New York to play with the Fletcher Henderson Orchestra, the premier African American band of the time. There he met tenor sax player Coleman Hawkins, from Saint Joseph, Missouri; Armstrong's improvised solos would impress Hawkins, leading to his influence on younger generations of saxophone players. Louis's over-the-top style of playing and improvising challenged the other players to keep up.[28] During recording sessions, however, Henderson would not allow Armstrong to sing, other than the brief scat at the end of "Everybody Loves My Baby," marking his debut as a singer on a recording.[29]

Armstrong cut many records as a backup musician during this period, including with blues singers Ma Rainey, Bessie Smith, and Alberta Hunter. He would eventually go on to accompany female blues singers in over one hundred recordings.[30]

He returned to Chicago in 1925 and recorded with his own bands, the Hot Five and Hot Seven, for the Okeh record label. These bands, consisting of musicians that included Johnny St. Cyr (banjo), Johnny Dodds (clarinet), Kid Ory (trombone), and wife Lil on piano, were formed for the purposes of recording only, and he continued to perform as a member of bands led by others.

Louis with the King Oliver's
Creole Jazz Band in 1923
in Chicago. From left to
right: Honore Dutrey, Oliver,
Armstrong, Bill Johnson.

King Oliver och Bill Johnson bakom Honore Dutray
och den unge Louis Armstrong i Chicago 1923.

In the spread from one of his scrapbooks. Satchmo honors his time spent making *Glory Alley* in 1952, where, rather than playing himself as he usually did, he played Shadow Johnson, albeit oddly familiar, a horn player in New Orleans.

Across the spread he recalls his real roots, collaging a photo of his time spent with King Oliver and Lil Hardin from 1922 to 1923. From left to right: Johhny Dodds, Baby Dodds, Honore Dutrey, Armstrong, Joe Oliver, second wife Lil Hardin, and Bill Johnson. He punctuates this with mostly celebrity quotes and a headline declaring "Better Than Anything I Ever Had,"which is cut into the shape of a lascivious arrow.

Dance director Charles O'Curran demonstrates gestures Armstrong is to use in singing scene in street.

GLORY ALLEY

uis Armstrong has his biggest acting role in movie with New Orleans setting

Clowning behind the scenes during filming of picture, *Glory Alley,* trumpeter Louis Armstrong is cooled with seltzer by actor Ralph Meeker in gag photo.

AFFABLE, versatile trumpet king Louis Armstrong has been featured in some seven major Hollywood movies since his film debut back in 1930, but always as a musician. In his newest picture, however, he is cast in a semi-dramatic role in the forthcoming MGM melodrama, *Glory Alley,* a story about the ups and downs of a promising young prize fighter.

In the original screen play by Art Cohn, Armstrong has the part of Shadow Johnson, a jovial handyman at the Punch Bowl Bar and a close pal of Socks Barbarosa (Ralph Meeker), the "hottest fighter to come out of the South in 20 years." Setting for the movie is a colorful sector of New Orleans with an appropriate background of Dixieland music which affords Louis ample opportunity to blow his famed horn and to sing in his raspy but infectious style. He croons three tunes, *It's A Most Unusual Day, That's What The Man Said* and *Glory Alley.*

Musically and dramatically, Armstrong has a fat part in *Glory Alley,* but he is none too enthusiastic about his performance as an actor. "Clark Gable has nothing to worry about from me in competition on the screen," he humorously observes.

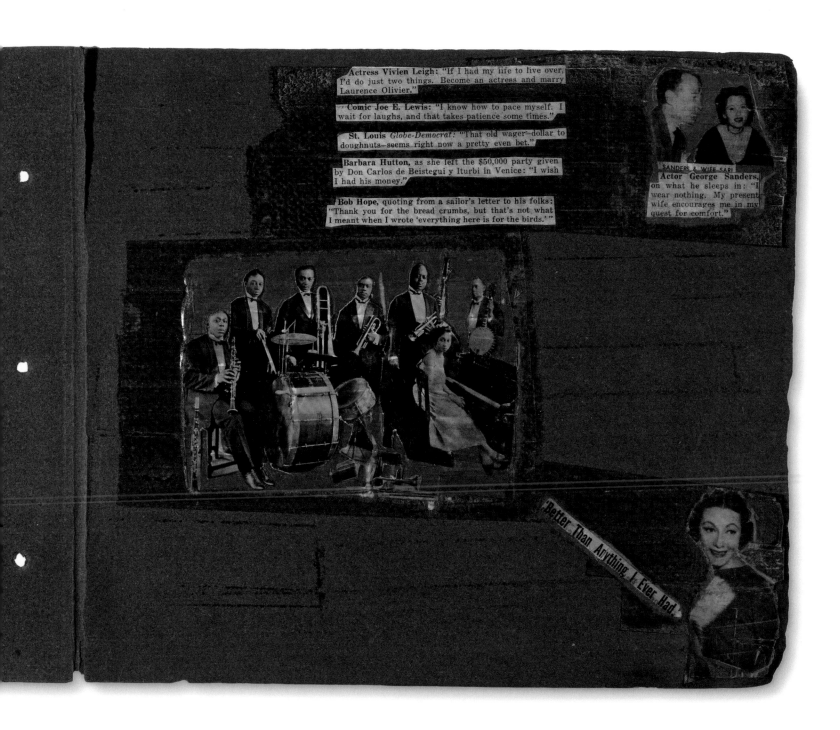

Actress **Vivien Leigh:** "If I had my life to live over, I'd do just two things. Become an actress and marry Laurence Olivier."

Comic **Joe E. Lewis:** "I know how to pace myself. I wait for laughs, and that takes patience some times."

St. Louis *Globe-Democrat:* "That old wager—dollar to doughnuts—seems right now a pretty even bet."

Barbara Hutton, as she left the $50,000 party given by Don Carlos de Beistegui y Iturbi in Venice: "I wish I had his money."

Bob Hope, quoting from a sailor's letter to his folks: "Thank you for the bread crumbs, but that's not what I meant when I wrote 'everything here is for the birds.'"

SANDERS & WIFE SARI
Actor George Sanders, on what he sleeps in: "I wear nothing. My present wife encourages me in my quest for comfort."

"Better Than Anything I Ever Had"

Below: A 78 rpm from Louis's personal collection, a reissue of his breakthrough 1920s recordings. The "recorded" label in Louis's hand denotes that he played this set into his reel-to-reel, most likely providing narration. This cover, designed by renowned Columbia Records art director Alex Steinwise, employs a collage portrait similar to Louis's own. **Right:** Another reissue of Louis's 78 rpm classic recordings, from 1941, also from his personal collection, illustration by Jim Flora.

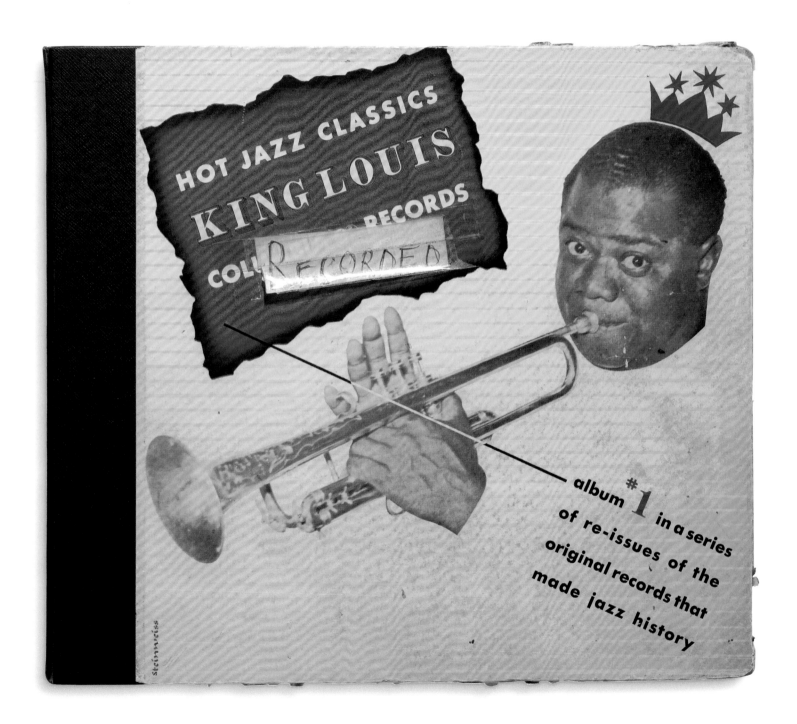

That is one reason why I never cared to be a band leader. Too much small pittance and catty things went on. I just wanted to blow my horn peacefully, the same as I am doing now.

—*Louis Armstrong[31]*

Louis also played with Erskine Tate's band, providing music for silent films, dance marathons, and live shows at the Vendome Theater in Chicago, and Armstrong broadened his repertoire to include jazz takes of classical songs, such as "Madame Butterfly."

Soon afterward he separated from Lil and joined the Carroll Dickerson Orchestra, featuring Earl Hines on piano, which in short order was renamed Louis Armstrong and His Stompers, although Hines continued to conduct. It was here that he first encountered Joe Glaser, who would later become his manager.

An indication of Louis's growing importance as early as 1927 was the publication of two books, *Louis Armstrong's 50 Hot Choruses for Cornet* and *Louis Armstrong's 125 Jazz Breaks for Cornet*, published by the Melrose Brothers Music Company in Chicago.

Returning to New York in 1929, he sang Fats Waller's "Ain't Misbehavin'" in the musical *Hot Chocolate*, stole the show, and had a bestseller with his recorded version of the song. Later that same year Armstrong recorded "I

Can't Give You Anything But Love, Baby" by Tin Pan Alley tunesmiths Dorothy Fields and Jimmy McHugh, the first of many times that Louis would take a popular song and recast it as his own. He lifted up everything he touched. It was an enormous success and one of his very last "race" records for Okeh.

His influence as a singer was felt by such mainstream crooners as Bing Crosby, and later Frank Sinatra, as well as jazz singers Billie Holiday and Nat King Cole.[32] Conversely, throughout his life, whenever Louis was questioned as to who his favorite musicians were, he would routinely reply Bing Crosby and Guy Lombardo.

His gravelly, apparently unschooled voice made him appealing to the masses in its disarming sincerity. Through an aural slight of hand, Louis made it sound easy, giving voice to the unsung. In reality he was subtly alternating melodies, changing lyrics and timing, leaving his stamp on all that he touched. Had he produced a more polished sound, he might not have found the wide audience he did. As it was, he would become a major star and remain a man of the people, significant, especially at the dawn of the Great Depression. Armstrong always wanted us to join in on the much-needed fun.[33] Highly likeable, he didn't take himself so seriously.

By the close of the decade Armstrong's status was that of a cultural hero and role model, especially among African Americans. His records sold internationally and his onstage patter and performances influenced an entire generation. His sartorial style was imitated and included a hairstyle known as "Louis Armstrong," which became popular with young men.

WITCH HAZEL AN COTTON ON SATCHMO'S CHOPS

To Jimmy Moran
a real Grand Guy - indeed
from
Louis Armstrong

Satchmo

He wore a tie that looked like an ascot tie with an extra big knot in it. Pops was the first to bring that style of knot to Los Angeles. Soon all the hip cats were wearing big knots in their ties. We called them **Louis Armstrong knots.**—*trumpeter Buck Clayton*

Like his hero Joe Oliver, Louis held a handkerchief at all times when performing. This soon became a trademark, and young fans would greet him with white handkerchiefs in hand, as a sign of deep affection.[34]

It is generally accepted that had Louis never played another note after the 1920s he still would be remembered as the single most creative and innovative force in jazz history.[35] But there was much, much more to come.

Louis and third wife Alpha.

1930s

Hobo, You Can't Ride That Train

The Satchmo Story.   2nd. Edition.

Side---1.

The first time that I smoked Marijuana (or) Gage as they so beautifly calls' it some time, was a couple of years after I had left Fletcher Henderson's Orchestra—playing at the Roseland in New York.. And returned to Chicago... It was actually in Chicago when I first picked my first stick of gage...And I'm telling you, I had myself a Ball...Thats' why it really puzzles me to see Marijuana connected with Norcotics—Dope and all that kind of crap...It is actually a shame. I was 26 years old then. And it never did impress me as dope. B......

In the spring of 1930, Louis made a pilgrimage by himself out to Los Angeles. He was soon hired by the West Coast Cotton Club to front their house band, where performances were regularly broadcast on radio. The following year, Louis appeared in his first Hollywood film, *Ex-Flame*, performing several songs.

Armstrong's impact on American culture is readily viewed through his flickering image on the silver screen. Beginning in the 1930s, racist stereotypes were applied to his visage, or at least attempted. Over time, Louis not only overcame the on-screen material, but by the 1950s was presented as a larger-than-life presence, and one that often possessed healing powers, who not only propelled the action, but solved problems from the myriad protagonists. Often he is referred to by a single nickname, "Louie." Ultimately he appeared in twenty-three American feature films as well as in numerous documentaries and foreign films.

One night between sets at the Cotton Club, Louis was arrested for the second time in his life, for marijuana possession, and spent nine days in jail. Rather than getting him blacklisted or hurting his career, the news of the arrest only helped to increase his notoriety.[36]

Louis remained an unrepentant advocate of marijuana use throughout his life. He thought of the drug as having beneficial mental and physical purgative properties, similar to the "physics" given to him by his mother to assure good health.[37]

In the summer of 1931, with Lil in tow, Louis made a triumphant return to New Orleans, an event covered by all the city papers. He visited the Colored Waifs' Home, now renamed the Municipal Boys' Home, and was photographed with the school's administrator, Captain Joseph Jones, and his former musical instructor and mentor, Peter Davis, along with the new boys' band. He also gladly posed with "Armstrong's Secret Nine," a black baseball team named after him.[38]

On July 9, 1932, Louis traveled to England with his new girlfriend, Alpha Smith (although still

Louis appeared regularly in newspapers, occasionally as the subject of a cartoon.

married to Lil Hardin), aboard the SS *Majestic*, to play the London Palladium, backed by a group of black Parisian musicians. As he was leaving the ship, an editor from *Melody Maker* magazine greeted him as "Satchmo," a shortening of his long-standing nickname "Satchelmouth." Armstrong liked what he heard and it became the favorite of his monikers. He played to mostly rave reviews, although in one he was described as "barbaric," and on stage was pelted with tomatoes.[38]

Afterward he returned to the States to tour. During this period Armstrong was besieged by managerial difficulties, with two claiming to represent him, and also began to experience chronic lip pain as the result of his intense performing schedule.

Satchmo would appear twice on the big screen in 1932. In a short movie, *A Rhapsody in Black and Blue*, he played a cleaning man who had been knocked out by his wife and dreamt of himself as the Emperor of Jazzmania.[39] He wakes up in an absurd set surrounded by his band and soap bubbles, dressed in an outlandish leopard-skin costume, apparently gone native, with bare chest exposed. Louis's performance overcame the racist material. With a devilish gleam in his eye and a defiant manner that transcended the setting, he sings (perhaps to the film's makers) "(I'll Be Glad When You're Dead) You Rascal You."

In a Betty Boop cartoon of the same name, Louis again must make the most out of racist material. Although this cartoon is bracketed with fine film performances of Armstrong leading his band, performing "High Society Rag," he is transformed in the body of the animation into a threatening floating head of an African native, singing "You Rascal You." During the filming of the opening and closing scenes Louis kept dancing out of camera range, and the producers finally had to draw chalk lines to keep him on camera.[40] Cab Calloway would fare somewhat better

later that year in his Betty Boop premier, where he was only morphed into a singing walrus.

On March 31, 1933, *London's Daily Express* reported "Man With Iron Lip Killed by His Art," stating that Louis "died suddenly in a nursing home in New York, a victim to the terrific strain which his art put on him."[41] To prove them wrong Louis returned to tour throughout Belgium, England, France, and Scandinavia.[42] Ten thousand people turned out at the Copenhagen rail station to greet him.

Hey, Louis Armstrong, how do you like our Swedish women? —*a fan*

Man, my wife has the best Smorgasbord in town."

—*Louis Armstrong*

While playing on stage in London at the Holborn Empire, his lip split, spewing blood all over his white tuxedo shirt. He was forced into a several month layoff as a result.[43]

My chops was beat, but I'm dyin' to swing again. —*Louis Armstrong*

Louis returned to the United States in January 1935 and did not play the trumpet again until that summer. He engaged Joe Glaser as his new manager, which would prove to be a relationship that would last for the rest of their lives.

In July 1935, he resumed touring throughout the Midwest and southern states with a fifteen-piece orchestra. Upon returning to New York City, Armstrong discovered many of the band members had union problems and were not able to play in the city.[44] He disbanded the group and agreed to play with the Luis

LOUIS ARMSTRONG
And His Famous Orchestra

Personal Management
JOE GLASER
R C A Building 30 Rockefeller Plaza
New York N. Y.

Louis in a movie still from
Pennies From Heaven in 1936,
his first of many outings with
Bing Crosby.

This spread: With the cast of *Dr. Rhythm* in 1938, appearing in yet another Bing Crosby vehicle.

"DOCTOR RHYTHM" with BING CROSBY, Mary Carlisle, Beatrice Lillie, Andy Devine, Laura Hope Crews, Rufe Davis.   An Emanuel Cohen Production.   A Paramount Picture   Made in U. S.

REEVES 427

"DOCTOR RHYTHM" with BING CROSBY.

"In case of defect in packaging, labeling or manufacturing this recording tape will be replaced. Except for such replacement, this recording tape is sold without warranty or any liability of any kind."

Russell Orchestra, broadcasting radio shows from Connie's Inn four times per week. The Luis Russell Orchestra was soon renamed Louis Armstrong and His Orchestra and proved extremely popular, recording and touring for the next decade.[45] It was during this period that the big band swing era emerged, as exemplified by the white Benny Goodman, Tommy Dorsey, and Glenn Miller bands. In fact the impetus for this began years earlier, in the late 1920s and early 1930s, with the music played by black bands such as Duke Ellington's, Fletcher Henderson's, and Armstrong's.

Louis's first full-bodied big screen performances came next in 1936's *Pennies from Heaven*, an early Bing Crosby vehicle directed by Norman Z. McLeod and written by William Rankin, . Armstrong's character, Henry, first appears as a deferential farmhand, replete with straw between the teeth, as he readily agrees to become a chicken rustler along with his band to help save the farm (that is, a chicken restaurant situated in a "haunted house" on an expanse of farmland). He's next seen performing for the first evening's crowd, wearing a handsome double-breasted suit, mugging it up with the ghost-themed "Skeleton in the Closet." Still, the sequence is dramatically lit, and Armstrong steals the show, first in the course of singing with arms waving and then especially when he picks up his horn, literally casting a large shadow.

Next he leads the band as Crosby croons "Let's Call a Heart a Heart." We can actually witness Louis's influence on Crosby within these frames, as Crosby transforms from being a ballad crooner (the eponymous "Pennies from Heaven," "So Do It") to a jazz singer ("One Two Button Your Shoe") right before our eyes. Armstrong's exit is as abrupt as it began, with a surprising dive through a window during a police raid for the

chicken thieves. This exuberant brief appearance earned him fourth billing.

In this, his first character role, Louis was the very first African American to share top, equal billing with white actors. He also received equal billing with costars Frances Langford and Crosby on a 78 rpm hit record of the film's music.[46]

In August of 1937 Louis appeared in the film *Artists and Models* with Martha Raye. Raye's gyrations while Armstrong serenaded brought about reviews citing scandal, such as one in *Variety* criticizing the "intermingling of the races." As a result Glaser and Armstrong arrived at a formulaic approach to his screen appearances whereby he would appear as a musician, usually as himself, for a specialty number, with little or no interaction with women or much interaction with whites. This basic precept was continued for the majority of Louis's film career.[47] This paid off in the following year, as Armstrong received an Academy Award nomination for his performance in the film *Going Places*, directed by Ray Enright and cowritten by Sig Herzig. Louis once again had to make the most out of questionable material. As Gabe, a horse trainer, he sings "Jeepers Creepers" to Jeepers, the horse. As is typical, Louis's singing is so charming and heartfelt that even the horse is won over.[48]

Later in 1937 Armstrong substituted for Rudy Vallee for six weeks as the host of *The Fleischmann's Yeast Hour*, the first black person to host a nationally sponsored radio program. In 1938 he divorced Lil Hardin, from whom he had been separated for years, and married Alpha.

A kinetic collage and a kinetic pose from *Artists and Models*, 1937. Prevailing racist attitudes and negative reviews caused the scenes between Armstrong and Martha Raye to be cut when shown in the South.

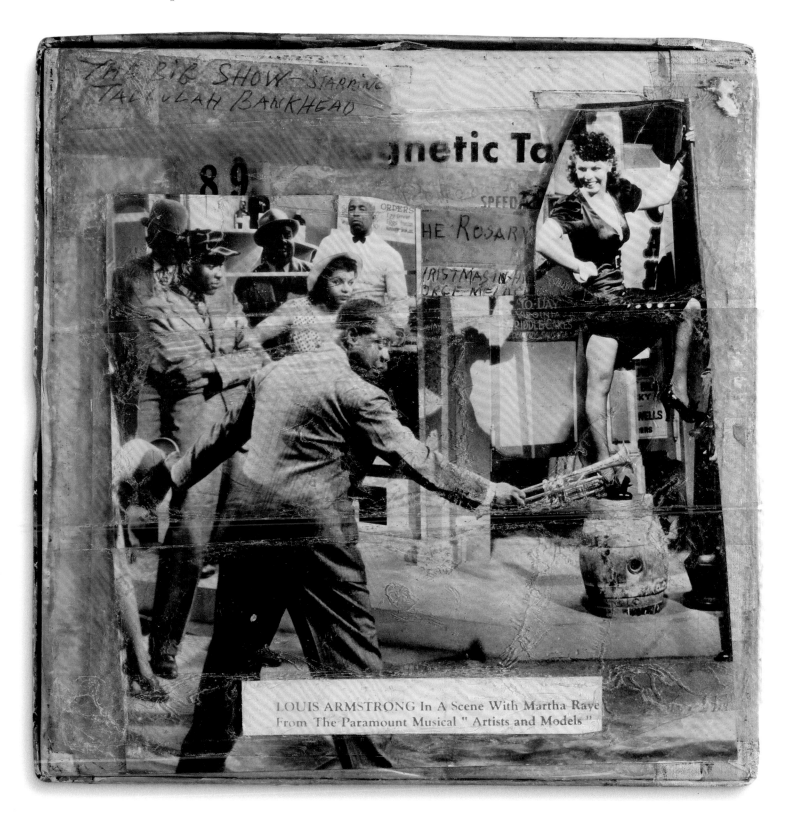

Another still from the film
Artists and Models. Directed by
esteemed director Raoul Walsh.
His scene with costar Martha
Raye stirred up a controversy
that affected the rest of
Louis's film career.

"ARTISTS AND MODELS" with Ida Lupino, Richard Arlen, Gail Patrick, Ben Blue, Judy Canova, The Yacht Club Boys, Louis Armstrong
Andre Kostelanetz and His Orchestra, Russell Patterson's "Personettes", Judy, Anne and Zeke, Connie Boswell.
A Paramount Picture

Louis decked out in tails. He makes the most of the red ground. Swiss Kriss is the laxative he promoted.

Alpha used to sit in the front row every time she came, and would sit right where I could get a good look at her. And she had big pretty eyes. Anyway, I couldn't keep from diggin' her. —*Louis Armstrong*

Talking on record about himself and his band, and singing songs about himself, as in the self-penned "Satchelmouth Swing" (Ol' Satchel's in the mood) helped to increase and spread his fame.

In 1937, Louis made an appearance in *Every Day's a Holiday*, a Mae West comedy directed by A. Edward Sutherland and written by West. Interacting with no one, Louis shows up wearing a pith helmet and white uniform, leading a parade, and sings "Jubilee," and his horn can be heard during the closing credits.

"We all do 'do, re, mi,' but you have to find the other notes yourself."—Louis Armstrong

1940s

Swing That Music

Louis's celebrity continued to grow and he performed in many films during this period, establishing many friendships with the stars of the day. Orson Welles, that enfant terrible of *Citizen Kane* fame, had a great desire to create a film tentatively titled *The Story of Jazz*, which would trace the history from its roots in New Orleans to its spreading around the world over four generations. Welles based much of the tale on Armstrong's experiences and completed a screenplay. Louis was to play a character, Reggie, clearly based on himself, who falls under the tutelage of an older musician, King Jeffers, based on Joe Oliver.

His character was to leave New Orleans and go to a music conservatory where he was to become a teacher, only to fall on hard times during the Depression.

Welles went so far as to audition Billie Holiday for a role, and placed both Duke Ellington and Armstrong on retainer. Lil Hardin was cast as a character in the film, but not herself, as she was deemed too old. That role went to actress Hazel Scott. Welles obtained a contract from music publisher Allen, Towne & Heath and filmed color footage of musical performances. Beleaguered by the unwillingness of RKO studio to support his creative

vision, Welles was eventually forced to drop the original idea and enlisted Louis to help create a straight-forward version of Armstrong's life, along with a concurrent jazz history.

However, by 1941 filming had begun on *The Magnificent Ambersons*, in which Welles applied the same technique of a narrative depicting historical change over several decades. He therefore abandoned the jazz film. Rather than give up on the project completely, Welles considered combining the footage already shot with the documentary he was simultaneously working on, *It's All True*.[49]

Welles's well-publicized trouble with RKO brought that project to a halt as well. However, in 1945 Welles visited Armstrong backstage and the two revived their interest in the project. Louis supplied Welles with a lengthy synopsis of his life, one of several he would write over time.

Screenwriter Elliot Paul, who worked on a treatment of this version with Welles (although Orson denied it) took the idea to producer Jules Levey. Armstrong was rehired for the newly configured film, but Welles was left in the dust, as was Louis's factual history.

The film was released as *New Orleans* in April of 1947, directed by Arthur Lubin and cowritten by Elliot Paul and Herbert J. Biberman, barely recognizable as the film Welles envisioned. Still, it costarred many greats from New Orleans, including Kid Ory, "Zutty" Singleton, "Barney" Bigard, and Charlie Beal.

Ella Fitzgerald and Satchmo set
the tone for this joyful collage
punctuated by tape and negative
space. She was his frequent
collaborator and duet partner,
beginning in 1946.

"Every note Louis hit was perfection." —Hoagy Carmichael

ELLA AND SATCHMO

Lucille Wilson, Louis's fourth wife, whom he wed in 1942, as a Cotton Club dancer in 1936. They were married for close to thirty years.

Dark Dancer

Lucille Wilson will dance in the "Blackbirds 1936" show at the Gaiety Theatre on Thursday.

Louis and Lucille's Corona home, purchased in 1943, punctuates this melodic collage. They would reside there for the rest of their lives. Elsewhere Louis and All-Star bandmate and friend Jack Teagarden perform.

The background line art, Louis's handwriting, and the natty attire give this collage a true Jazz Age feel.

Louis celebrates international publisher Leeds Music transcribing his solos. He was first so honored in 1927 with the publication of *Louis Armstrong's* *50 Hot Choruses for Cornet* and *Louis Armstrong's 125 Jazz Breaks for Cornet*, published by the Melrose Brothers Music Company in Chicago.

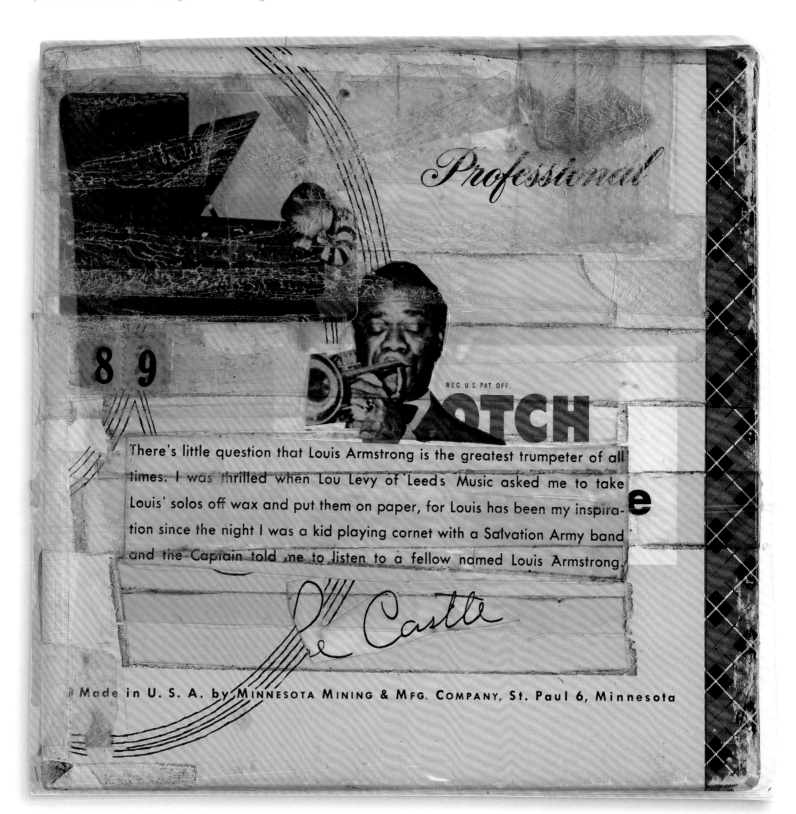

There's little question that Louis Armstrong is the greatest trumpeter of all times. I was thrilled when Lou Levy of Leeds Music asked me to take Louis' solos off wax and put them on paper, for Louis has been my inspiration since the night I was a kid playing cornet with a Salvation Army band and the Captain told me to listen to a fellow named Louis Armstrong.

The inside cloth binding provided Louis with a colorful ground on which to create. Covering decades' worth of subject matter, he whimsically displays a famous "Cake Walk" performer from the turn of the century, as well as author Alexandre Dumas, Lucille, and sheet music for a beer jingle. A cake walk was an African American satirical parody of the formal European ballroom dances preferred by white slave owners.

Opposite are a trio of membership cards to various organizations, and a telling quote: "It's great to be great, it's greater to be human," which sums up Satchmo's positive and egalitarian philosophy.

This Certifies that

Louis Armstrong

IS A MEMBER OF THE

"MELODY LAINERS" FAN CLUB

For One Year From *Honorary* To *Member*
AND IS ENTITLED TO ALL CLUB PRIVILEGES.

Pat Porter   *Arlene Shay*

The American Legion

PARIS POST N° 1   DEPT. OF FRANCE

HONORARY GUEST CARD

AS A TOKEN OF OUR PERSONAL APPRECIATION

THIS TESTIMONIAL IS PRESENTED TO

Lonsieur Louis ARMSTRONG

HOT CLUB DE FRANCE

(FÉDÉRATION FRANÇAISE DES HOT CLUBS)

Fondé en 1932

Président d'Honneur : Louis ARMSTRONG
Siège : 14 Rue Chaptal, PARIS-9°

HOT CLUB de   MARSEILLE   N° 154

Nom
Adresse

Le Président du H. C. F.,   Le Président,   Le Titulaire,

WESTERN UNION

CK PD KANS CITY MO 855 PM AUG 4 1952

LOUIS ARMSTRONG

WOBERLY MO

THANKS FOR EVERTHING AST NIGHT LISTENING TO YOUR PASADENA CONCERT

NOW YOUR STILL THE GRATEST LET US HEAR FROM YOU

JACK AND MERIAM ROSS   1230 AM

Put on your glasses,

"It Is Great To Be Great,
But It's Greater To Be Human"

That's when I stopped her
from Talking by slowly
reaching for her Cute little
Beautifiulled Manicured
hand! And said to her,
Can you Cook 'Red Beans
And Rice? Which Amused
her very much. Then it dawned
her on that I'very Serious.
she—being A northern girl BORN IN N.Y.C
And ME Southern boy? FROM N.O'
She Could see why I Asked
her that Question. So She
said! I've never Cooked that
Kind of food before, But—

Just give me a little time too
and I think that I can fix
it for you. That's all that
I wanted to hear, and right
away I said, how about
Inviting me out to your
house for dinner tomorrow
night? She said, wait a
minute, give me time to
get it together, as my wits
together, or somphting,
we'll, in a couple of days
from now? Gladly I
accepted. Two days later
I was at her house on time

The film *New Orleans* was a highly fictionalized version of the history of New Orleans jazz and played loose with the facts. Still, Louis was seen throughout, and has much screen time. Billie Holliday played his love interest, Endie, and together and apart they turned in fine performances. Importantly, the film is about not only the racist conditions that existed during the time period in which it is set, the late teens and early twenties, but indeed those that still existed when the film was made in 1947.

The title song became a standard for Armstrong, and there is much music throughout, including "Where the Blues Were Born in New Orleans," "Buddy Bolden's Blues," "Farewell to Storyville," "The Blues Are Brewin'," and "Endie."

The film received mostly poor reviews, with the exception of accolades for the jazz performances, particularly Armstrong's:

> **Put it down as a fizzle in every respect but one. That is the frequent tooting of Louis Armstrong and his horn. When the old Satchmo blasts upon his trumpet, it is music to strong and durable ears.**
> —*The New York Times*[50]

In an article by D. Leon Wolff in the August 1941 issue of *Music & Rhythm* magazine, the writer declared: "Louis Armstrong Stopped Being God Back in 1932," claiming, "He lags technically and creatively by today's standards." That piece was accompanied by a still photograph from the Bing Crosby vehicle *Pennies from Heaven* (1936), a photo of a wide-eyed Louis performing

with a dancing skeleton. Although an indication of the shifting musical mood, this declaration would prove over time to be hyperbole, although it is significant that the author begrudgingly had to admit that Armstrong was once "God."

During the war years Armstrong continued to tour from coast to coast. In 1942 he divorced Alpha and married Lucille Wilson, a Cotton Club dancer who remained his wife for the rest of Armstrong's life.

> **[Actor] Raymond Massey, I think he's one of the greatest. When he played *Abe Lincoln in Illinois* on Broadway, ladies and gentleman, he got so carried away, after his last performance, he went up in Harlem and freed the Cotton Club girls.**
> —*Louis Armstrong*

Louis was playing as many as three hundred dates per year, and during most of his adult life he had lived out of suitcases in hotel rooms. Lucille decided to change all that, and in 1943 purchased a three-story brick-facade home in Corona, Queens, without Louis having seen it. Coming off tour, he told his wife to meet him outside, that he would take a cab and drive by the house, and if he didn't like what he saw he would keep going. When he arrived by cab, Lucille was nowhere in sight. He told the cabdriver to wait.

> **I got up enough courage to get out of the cab and rang the bell. And sure enough the door opened and who stood in the doorway with a real thin nightgown, and her hair in curlers?** —*Louis Armstrong*

After Lucille gave Louis a tour of the home, Louis invited the cab driver to dinner.[51]

In 1943 in the film adaptation of the Broadway show written by Lynn Root, *Cabin in the Sky*, directed by Vincente Minnelli, Satchmo played a mischievous character that was a member of "Lucifer Jr.'s" gang. The all African American cast starred Ethel Waters, Eddie "Rochester" Anderson, and Lena Horn. Sadly Louis's only song, "Ain't It the Truth," didn't make the final cut and the footage was lost or destroyed.

In 1947 Louis formed the All-Stars featuring old friends trombonist Jack Teagarden and Earl "Fatha" Hines. Louis Armstrong and his All-Stars soon became the highest-paid band in jazz. A fully integrated band, they were unable to perform in Louis's hometown of New Orleans, as well as many other places throughout the country. At a Carnegie Hall concert New York's *Daily News* wrote, "He doesn't drive with his trumpet quite as hard as he used to. But his veiled tone, the true melody of his breaks, and turns, and the musical good humor and sentiment of his phrasing are as beautiful today as they were when he was twenty years ahead of his time." *Down Beat* declared, "Nearly everyone agrees that Louis Armstrong is the outstanding figure in the history of jazz. The greatest trumpeter, the greatest vocalist, the greatest showman, the greatest influence, just the greatest."[52]

Well, not everyone. The beboppers, led by a new generation of horn players, like Dizzy Gillespie and Charlie Parker, would become openly critical of Armstrong, both his playing and onstage antics.[53] Armstrong uncharacteristically responded in kind, initially disapproving of both the style of music and the musicians who played it. Eventually both sides mellowed. At the Hollywood Bowl in 1952 Louis good-naturedly parodied bebop, sporting a golf cap with a pom-pom

on top, singing "Bye Bye Bebop" to the tune of "Bye Bye Blackbird":

**Every riff those cats make,
They think it's a gem,
So lord have mercy on all of them.**

"If it hadn't been for him, there would have been none of us. I want to thank Mr. Louis Armstrong for my livelihood," said Dizzy Gillespie. And Miles Davis agreed: "Louis has been through all kinds of styles. You know you can't play anything on a horn Louis hasn't played."[54]

Gillespie and Satchmo jammed together on *The Jackie Gleason Show*, Armstrong pushing Dizzie harder and higher in playful camaraderie.

A much greater controversy was brewing during Mardi Gras in New Orleans in 1949.

There's a thing I've dreamed of all my life, and I'll be damned if it don't look like it's about to come true—to be King of the Zulus Parade. After that, I'll be ready to die.

—Louis Armstrong

Indeed, back in 1926 Armstrong had recorded a tune entitled "King of the Zulus" written by Lil Hardin, with his Hot Five. His dream realized, Louis appeared in the parade as King of the Zulus, in the chalked face and white paint around his lips and eyes of minstrelsy. What was widely misunderstood outside his hometown was that the Zulus were actually parodying the white "king" Rex, a longstanding New Orleans tradition who appeared in racist blackface.

"Man, if you gotta ask, you'll never know." (response when asked to define jazz)—Louis Armstrong

Armstrong on the set of *A Song Is Born*, 1948, with costar Steve Cochran, who played the heavy in the film.

Billie Holiday apparently doesn't
like what she hears.

Louis was quite proud of his appearance as King of the Zulus in 1949, despite widespread criticism, the satirical nature of the events outside of native New Orleans lost on a wider audience. Here he lists every Zulu "King" and "Queen" right up to his "reign," and displays his membership card.

Opposite he creates an illustration out of wrapping paper, handwritten notes, and a greeting card, apparently from actress and dancer Leslie Caron, his costar in *Glory Alley*, noted in a Hawaiian clipping on his way to a European tour.

HAPPY NEW YEARS CARD FROM "GASSUH"

LESLIE CARON.

Happy NEW YEAR

WISHING YOU
all the really good things
A truly happy
New Year brings

HONOLULU.

"Hawaiian Hospitality"

Satchmo just finished making a movie called "Glory Alley" for Metro-Goldwyn-Mayer with Leslie Caron, French ballerina whose path he just missed crossing here. He leaves September 22 for his ninth tour of Europe, where he is grand presidente of "Le Jazz Hot,"

[Rex would] get off his big, fine boat looking like a million, which most of them have, so Zulu arrives by a rowboat named the royal barge. Each member has a burlesque of some character they have in mind.

—*Louis Armstrong*[55]

This one's for you, Rex.

—*Armstrong onstage in England, to members of the royal family, ignoring the rule that performers are not supposed to address them*

Perhaps Louis's desire to participate was personal was well. Louis rarely saw his father growing up, but would view him on the back of horse-drawn wagons during parades as grand marshal. And one of his many "stepfathers" (as his mother referred to her many suitors) had appeared king of the Zulus twenty

years before.[56] Still, there was considerable fallout from this appearance and it would follow Louis for years to come.

The previous year Louis had starred in *A Song Is Born*, his first film starring Danny Kaye. Louis appeared once again as himself, performing seated, in a crowded, rollicking nightclub, alongside Lionel Hampton on vibes, in one of Satchmo's most rousing appearances in a big Hollywood movie. The movie was written by no less than Billy Wilder (and Thomas Monroe), directed by Howard Hawks, and filmed by *Citizen Kane* alumnus Greg Toland with fast-cut tight shots of the swinging club patrons. Benny Goodman is the only one of the several musicians on hand to play a role rather than appear as himself. The Golden Gate Quartet turned in some fine performances, as did Tommy Dorsey. Louis is onscreen all the way through, alongside myriad other musicians. The whole affair ends with a jam session on Hampton's "Flying Home," sending the film out in style.

1950s

High Society

THE COLLAGES

Although he was still touring continually during this period, Armstrong began two new hobbies simultaneously: He would spend hours talking into a reel-to-reel tape recorder in his home, playing both his own records and eclectic recordings as well, including classical music and opera, commenting and reminiscing. He would then adorn the mostly 7-inch square tape boxes front and back with collages, culled from newspaper and magazine clippings, movie stills and photographs, holiday cards and telegrams, even occasional hand lettering, creating the visual equivalent to the aural record he was leaving behind. He had much grist for the mill, as next to Marilyn Monroe he is considered to be one of the most photographed persons of the twentieth century. He would then "laminate" the end result with Scotch tape, although he occasionally employed masking and white medical tape as well. He would also collage in several scrapbooks, using those to create a visual narrative about African American life and accomplishments, his career, and Hollywood. For someone who declared himself steadfastly nonpolitical, these pages stand in direct contradiction to that assertion.

How Armstrong arrived at collage is unknown,

or exactly when, as he wrote little of this endeavor. It is quite obvious that he brought the same exuberant joy to the visual arts as he did to all his creative undertakings. His choice of collage was a perfect fit, at once "high" art and "folk" art, the most jazzlike of all visual art forms, where he could take an existing theme and riff on it, decomposing and recomposing along the way. Many of these collages are quite rhythmic, leading one's eye in a playful manner, and often the main subject is himself, a form of self-portraiture. One feels Louis's lively sensibility, spontaneity, and intuition in these works, as well as his great warmth, passion, and love of others.[57]

Just as jazz, as it eventually came to be known, had grown out of "ragging" a tune—taking a known melody and playing something new on top of it—Louis would create a new visual diary out of found art.[58] And as he made variations with his horn, adding to and filling in the melody, and also riffed with words on paper, he now experienced the same freedom in collage art, shaking things up and putting them back together into something entirely new.[59]

As he had done throughout his career, he was creating at once a self-aware art form and a record of the events themselves, much the way he had introduced talking about band members and himself on vinyl years earlier. They not only stand in recognition of his celebrity, but by portraying fans alongside household names, are another testament to the great humility and generosity of the man. Indeed over the years Louis gave away a fortune in cash and gifts.[60]

This beautiful, elegant collage from 1970 dispels any notion that Armstrong simply created them as a mnemonic device. The objects on the left reflect the tree contained in the scrap on the right, and the color choices are deliberate and delicate.

The reverse side reveals itself to
be a birthday greeting to Lucille
from Astrid.

His voluminous creative output included around six hundred and fifty such recordings, with as many as five hundred collages adorning the cardboard boxes, pouring as much originality into his visual work as anything else he created.

Would Armstrong have opted to be a visual artist if given the opportunity? It is doubtful, as it would have been too introverted and solitary a life. He was, after all, a performer, an extrovert with a great capacity to love and a need to be loved.

It is no coincidence that collage had gained in popularity during the twentieth century. True, its roots could be traced back to ancient Japan, and examples exist during the thirteenth century in Persia, spreading to Turkey and eventually Europe by the 1600s. But the modern version that captured the public's attention was created in 1912, when Pablo Picasso first glued newspaper into a Cubist painting. It is noteworthy to mention that Picasso was greatly influenced by African art, and that that continent informed two emerging art forms at once, one visual and the other musical, joined together in their modernity.

Also unknown is whether Armstrong intended these collages for the public or private enjoyment. He would send the boxes as gifts to friends and fans alike. His love of collage spilled onto the walls and ceiling of his den, something Louis took great pride in—once again his larger-than-life personality and artistic vision too great to be contained within a small space—until Lucille forced him to take it all down.

There is no doubt that Louis was aware of the art world when he began creating collages. The list of artists who recreated his countenance, or used his music as a source of inspiration, is staggering: Romare Bearden, René Bouché, Paul Colin, Miguel Covarrubias, Stuart Davis, Charles Delaunay, Charles Demuth, Arthur Dove, Francis Feist, Palmer Hayden, Al Hirschfeld, Franz Kline,

Jacob Lawrence, Stephen Longstreet, Reginald Marsh, Archibald Motley, Jr., LeRoy Neiman, Ralph van Lehmden, Jules Pascin, Winold Reiss, Misha Reznikoff, Ben Shahn, Blanding Sloan, and Stokely Webster.[61]

Some attest that the collages were made simply for his personal satisfaction, to serve as a memory aid, and that he didn't take them all that seriously.

> **[Louis was always] carrying a pair of scissors around with him and constantly cutting up newspapers, _Jet_ and _Life_ magazines and anything he wanted to remember. He would cut out pictures, words, headlines, etc. and paste them all into notebooks that he carried around. It was a hobby of his. We'd see him in between sets—cutting and pasting these bits together.**
> —_band member Marty Napoleon_

However, this would not explain the hundreds of collages Armstrong passionately produced for more than fifteen years.[62] They were important enough to Louis that he solicited materials from others, while referring to it as a hobby:

> **I guess you've wondered why all the regalia [the photo] that I sent you . . . huh? Well, you know, my hobbie (one of them anyway) is using a lot of scotch tape . . . .** —_Louis Armstrong_

As he did with his writing, Louis recorded his personal history and travels, adding to his own myth. Everything about the man was larger than life: his outgoing

Louis rehearses on the set of *The Five Pennies* with Danny Kaye and Susan Gordon. Kaye portrayed trumpet player and bandleader Red Nichols. It was widely rumored that Satchmo played Kaye's horn parts on the sound track, but in reality it was Nichols himself.

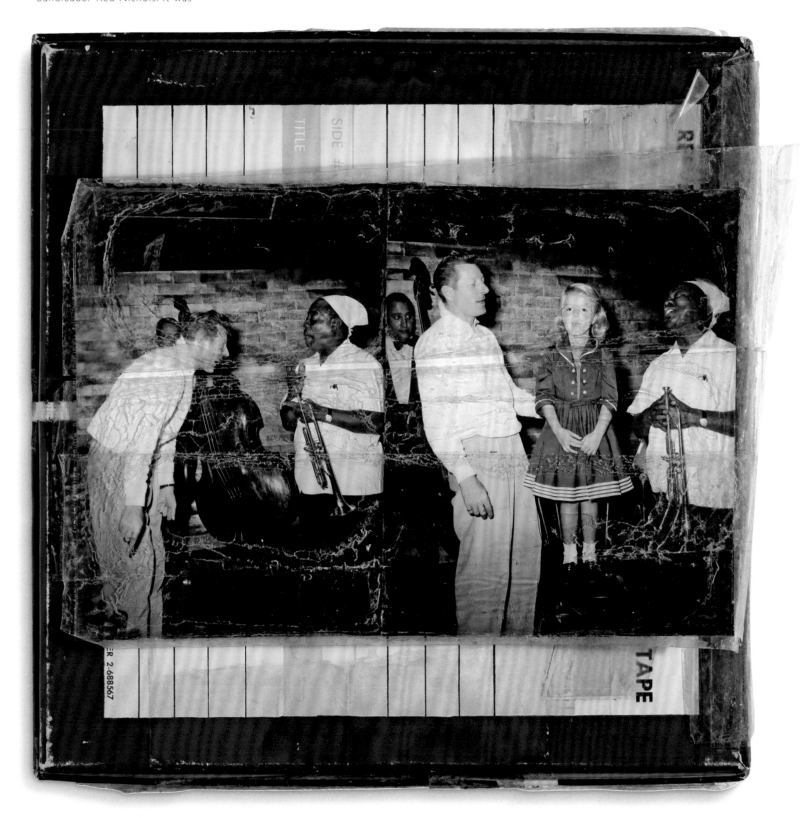

A rare example of Louis creating an illustration, a trumpet out of wrapping paper, carefully arranging the printed designs to form the bell, mouthpiece, and valves. Eccentric as ever, he decorates this with copy about Swiss Kriss.

A lyrical collage created from
greeting cards.

Trummy Young during the All-Stars' triumphant tour of West Africa. Over one hundred thousand attended his concert in Accra.

"I feel at home in Africa. I'm African-descended down to the bone, and I dig the friendly ways these people go about things.—Louis Armstrong

Louis shares equal billing with
"the lady who makes Swiss Kriss."

In this multilayer collage, Louis
appears in the foreground as
well as the background.

This playful collage features
Lucille and Louis, and pianist
and composer Clarence Williams
wearing a tie that Satchmo
turned into a portrait of Velma

Middleton, his singing and
performing companion from the
All-Stars.

Louis celebrates his own
artistry, in this rare collage
with hand lettering.

Satchmo poses with two fans apparently explaining "how to listen to music."

Below: Lucille honored Louis in his birthday in 1958, and Louis returned the favor, creating a collage from her greeting card and signature, and a photo where he looks lovingly her way.
Right: A single word, "JAZZ," sums it all up.

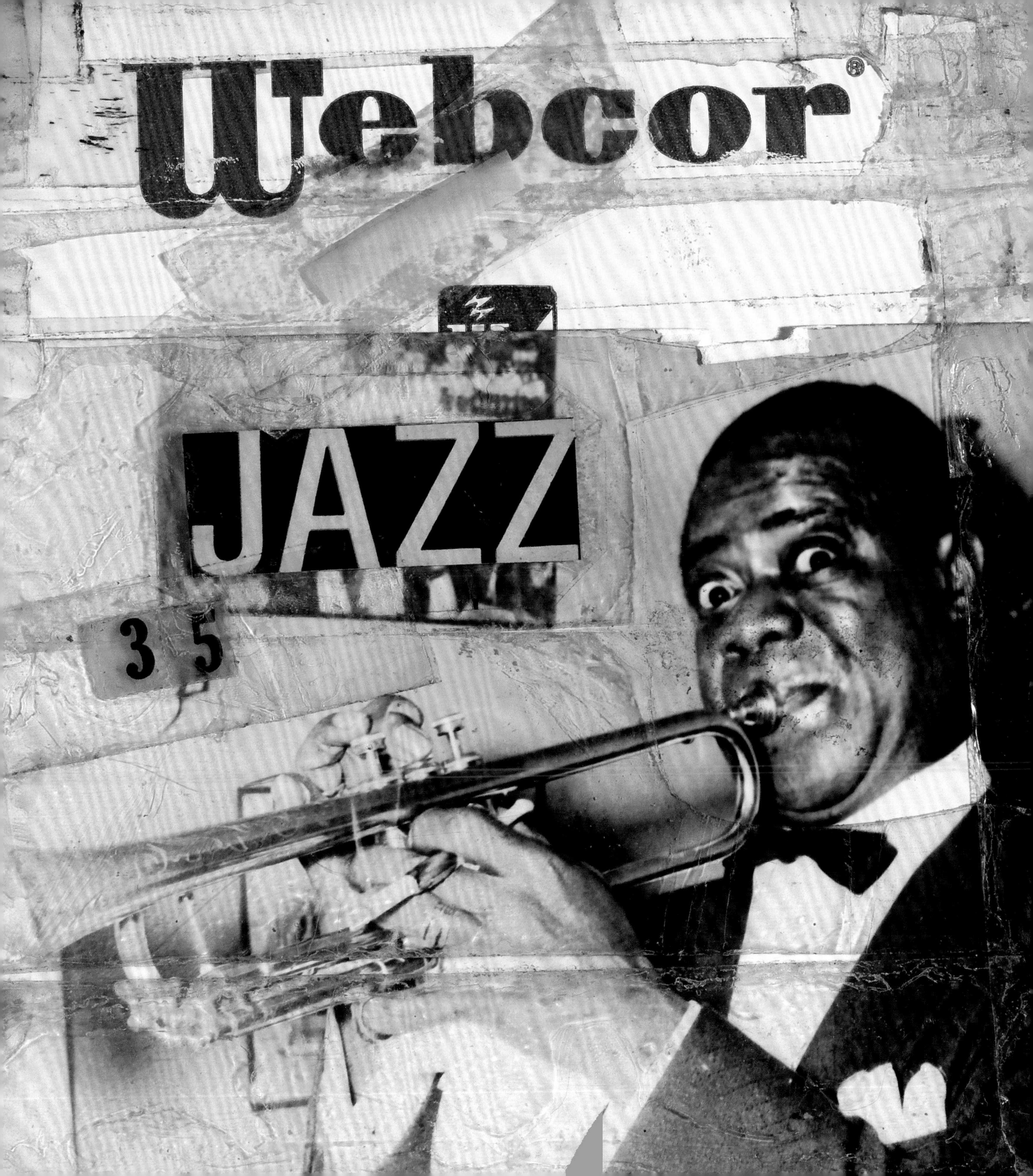
Webcor®
JAZZ
35

In the left photo Satchmo "jams"
with Danny Kaye as Red Nichols
in the film *The Five Pennies*.

Satchmo and trombonist Trummy
Young wail a duet.

The words "Welcome Home"
are repeated twice, perhaps in
contrast or accord with this
image of Louis being made up
for film.

On the reverse side we view the
entire set of *Glory Alley*. The pensive
look on Louis's face denotes how
seriously he took his acting.

In separate photos, Louis and Lucille pose with a young fan. Top and bottom are photographs of the wall collages Louis created. Featured on the walls are not only jazz greats Ella Fitzgerald, Duke Ellington, Ornette Coleman, as well as myriad photos of himself, but also folk and blues great Huddie "Leadbelly" Ledbetter.

Louis blows (or pretends to blow) on the set of *Glory Alley*.

"If you don't like Louis Armstrong, you don't know how to love." —Mahalia Jackson

Reel No. 5 5

A loving portrait of his adopted
son Clarence Armstrong.

Louis's younger sister "Mama Lucy," a.k.a. Beatrice.

Satchmo awards himself a well-deserved and long-overdue doctorate in jazz.

"Happy New Year" wished via telegram from Robert E. Kintner, the pioneering television executive who was instrumental in shaping the development of two of the major networks, ABC and NBC.

Louis takes over and makes the
most out of existing art.

"JAZZMASTER"

Louis goes uptown "at the
opera" for a recording
of classical music.

Louis looks uncharacteristically
pensive. Horn player Mezz
Mezzrow is seen center,
shaking hands.

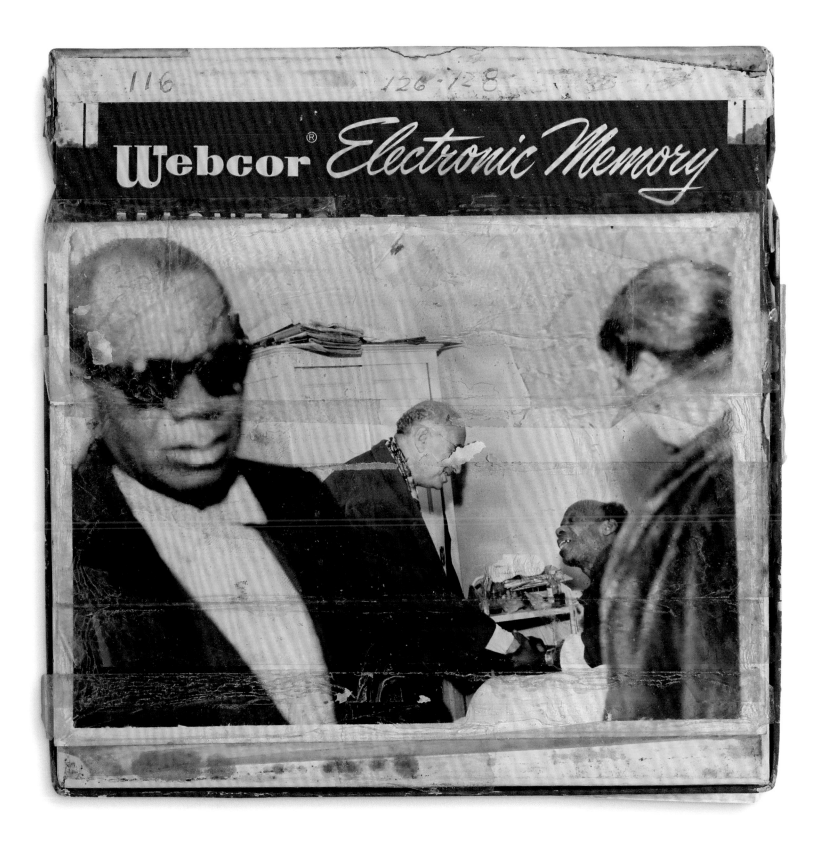

In one of his more perceptibly musical works, Louis combines a photograph of his seventy-eight albums with publicity photos, records, and cutout heads of himself, Al "Jazzbo" Collins, and an undentified woman. The setup and composition lead the eye counterclockwise from top to bottom and back to the albums.

Louis composes with photographs
and medical tape.

Placement on negative space adds
to the musicality of this effort
showcasing Mr. and Mrs. Glaser.

A beautifully composed collage makes the most of Scotch tape, labels, and color photography featuring, humorously, "Satchmo and his fan."

"All we can do is be glad we live in the same century as Louis Armstrong." —Wynton Marsalis

Spencer Tracy, an unidentified
woman, and Louis.

Louis with Velma Middleton.
Inset is horn player Muggsy
Spanier on the left.

In a serious mood.

SCOTCH Magnetic Tape

Louis sits with fans.

"There never was any hidden side to him. He came 'as is.'" —All Stars clarinetist Barney Bigard

Louis decorated a tape of
calypso musician and singer
Harry Belafonte with an
incongruous image from his
own stage performance.

Louis plays a collage-only duet
with clarinetist Barney Bigard.

In a visual slight of hand Satchmo appears to be jamming with, from left to right, Edmond Hall, Irving "Mouse" Randolph, and Henderson Chambers, who were part of the 1947 concert at Carnegie Hall. It was rare that Louis had a second trumpet play with him. Since there is a hint of the same music stand in the photo of Louis, these two images may indeed have been taken at the same session, or are the same photograph that he then cut.

"Louis Armstrong was the epitome of jazz and always will be."—*Duke Ellington*

On the back he jams for real
with Trummy Young.

Louis and Dottie Hansen share
a typical pose. She was the host
of the teen dance show *Dottie
Hansen's Hi-Time*.

A night out on the town.

Sharing a happy feeling with
friends and fans.

With young fans, and beneath,
carefully trimmed typography.

Louis and his fans regularly
crossed genres.

During a radio interview the host and Louis examine artwork featuring—who else—Louis!

Louis looks uncharacteristically
tired as he autographs a book.

Louis combines several controversies in a single collage: The judge who signed an injunction to prevent Arkansas's Governor Faubus from blocking integration; a photo of the aftermath of seven thousand German music fans who were driven so wild by Louis playing that they overturned chairs; Satchmo criticizing bebop, "After forty-five minutes, [the] song is familiar."

"I don't let my mouth say nothin' my head can't stand." —Louis Armstrong

Louis and the All-Stars jam with
jazz fiddler Stefan Grapelli.

"My whole life, my whole soul, my whole spirit is to blow that horn." —Louis Armstrong

A portrait of Beryl Bryden, an English jazz singer. Armstrong misspells her first name. Ella Fitzgerald called her "Britain's queen of the blues."

Louis surrounded by young fans.

Louis Armstrong

Foto: Metro-Goldwyn-Ma   Rüdel-Verlag

AUDIO DEVICES, In   dison Ave., New York 22, N.Y.

Louis regales the crowd.

Louis is placed on a pedestal and
crowned king, in absentia.

Like the opening four bars of
a song, Armstrong creates four
visual notes using differing tones
of photos, concluding with him
packed and ready to go.

On the reverse side he adds two
more notes.

Two of the things Louis enjoys:
playing onstage (with Jack
Teagarden) and eating, in this
less-is-more composition.

Louis surrounds his portrait in
textures of white.

Louis enjoys a moment at
the Saint Germain-des Prés
café in Paris.

All-Star trombonist Tyree
Glenn works out.

Louis signs a copy of the French edition of *My Life in New Orleans*. **Right:** Pearl Bailey and Louis double-billed in Las Vegas.

Reel "158" 23/4

INTERNATIONAL HOTEL
LAS VEGAS, NEVADA 89109

PEARL & LOUIS
BAILEY   ARMSTRONG

Made in U. S. A. by MINNESOTA MINING & MFG. COMPANY, St. Paul 6, Minnesota

the International brings the world to Las Vegas!

Louis with in front of the theater
where the All-Stars are playing.

The lively color reflects
Louis's mood, underscored
by the inset photo.

Left: Louis utilizes pre-existing art to create the illusion of hands holding a framed picture of a theater facade where he is performing alongside Gary Crosby, the son of his friend and frequent costar Bing Crosby.
Below: "When It's Sleepy Time Down South" co-composer Otis Rene wishes Louis well for an upcoming performance at the Hollywood Bowl.

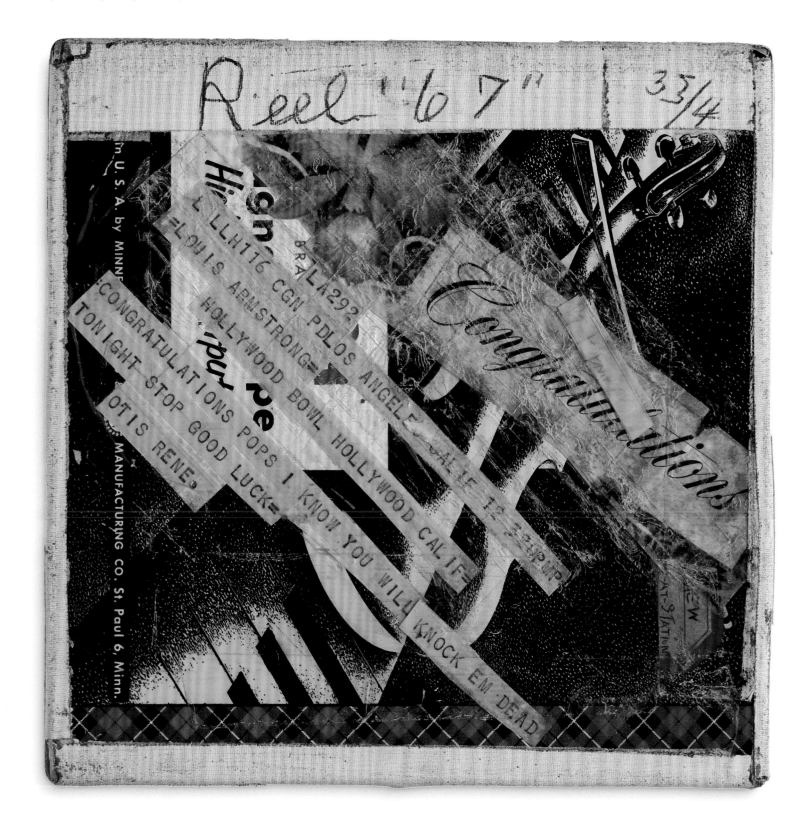

Louis drops his trousers to
promote Swiss Kriss. He sent this
out as a Christmas card! At the
bottom is Louis's own logotype.

A Swiss Kriss package is featured
right alongside the All-Stars.

An incredibly musical composition, the visual equivalent of seeing the All-Stars in concert. Pictured, left to right, are Velma Middleton, pianist Billy Kyle, clarinetist Barney Bigard, drummer Kenny Jones, bassist Milt Hilton, and trombonist Trummy Young.

Tape creates a rhythmic
pattern across photos of a
lively radio interview.

Louis backed up by a big band.

Louis looking quite serious
with Lucille (obscured) being
interviewed by Paloma Efrom in
Buenos Aires in 1957.

Louis collages the work of
another artist, de Radzitzky,
demonstrating his knowledge of
and appreciation for the form.

Louis sings a cappella.

Louis employs bold hand
lettering and angles to create a
melodious rhythm.

On the left of this spread from his scrapbook Louis places floating heads of the band, Lucille, and the mayor of Honolulu, who presented keys to the city to Armstrong, above a lively letter penned by himself.

On the right Louis pays tribute to baseball great Jackie Robinson, the African American athlete who broke racial barriers in sports, much the same as Armstrong did in music.

DUSTY BROOKS
and his TONES

**FORWARDED TO YOU
FROM HONOLULU, HAWAII**

SATCHMO

In Waikiki - 'Yea...

Honolulu,
February 29th, 1952,

Speaking of Heaven on Earth
Folks, don't let nobody-,fool-'you,
Because, Louis'Satchmo'Armstrong
Is, having himself a'Ball,
In Honolulu....... I'm 'Tellin, 'Yoo...

Mayor Wilson presented the keys of the city
to Louis "Ol Satchmo" Armstrong
and his wife

Aloha: all you Disc Jockeys and Newspaper, 'Cats,

This is Louis Armstrong, writing from the Grass Skirt Country...We are over here entertaining all the soldiers and these fine people here for a couple of weeks... And I'm
telling you, I, and my All Stars, are just about the happiest people in the world...
Even to my wife 'Lucille, and my fine manager Mr Joe Glaser... They too, said, the
people of Honolulu make you feel so much at home, until we can easily see now, why,
so many of the 'Cats, would give their right arm to stay much, much longer... And as
for, mee''-- I feel just like a Native already.... The way these Hawaiian kiddies
were putting those Lai,s, around my neck, the night I arrived into town, Hmmm...For
a moment, I thought I was a Jockey, just come from winning a big Race...Ha ha ha...
But it was kicks... Especially, to me and my Ol, Bashful'self....

Can you imagine,?..Everybody who 'Lay's a 'Lai' on ya' - gives, you a kiss. There
was en elderly fellow, who,s one of my stout record fans...He put a Lai,around my
neck, and gave me a ''Beeeg Kees... Between, he,needing a shave, and those beautifully smelling lais,(real cold-fresh-ones-) creeping around my neck, I'm tellin,
you, I was a thrilled 'Cat''....Even the babies, came up to the Cadillac,Ahem- that
Lucille and I were riding to our hotel in and put their little 'lais,around my neck
.... Wonderful, no foolin...

WELCOME TO HONOLULU

'OL SATCHMO' GETS KEY TO CITY

Most fans know this Robinson as he looks covering second at Ebbetts Field over in Brooklyn.

PAGE 17

Celebrities attended premier of Jackie's moving picture at Astor theater. Cab Calloway and his wife, "Nuffie," join Jackie and his wife Rachael in theater lobby before show.

At Pittsburgh, Aug. 24, 1948, Jack was tossed out of his first game by Butch Henline. Sukeforth(c) was put out too.

UCLA fans remember 20-year old Jackie Robinson as one of the fastest grid stars of 1939-1940.

The other woman in Jack's life is his mother, Mallie Robinson. Here she's visiting Jack and Rachael at St. Albans, L. I. She makes her home in Calif.

Left: A portrait of Louis is joined by several floating heads.
Right: Louis pays tribute to several musical greats: Duke Ellington, Bix Beiderbecke, Jack Teagarden, Jelly Roll Morton, Ruth Brown, drummer "Big" Sid Catlett, Broadway star Florence Mills, and President Franklin D. Roosevelt. Most significantly he places "King" Joe Oliver within his own consciousness. Throughout his life Louis would regard Oliver as his teacher and inspiration.

Louis pays homage to the African American "million dollars worth of talent" who work on Broadway: Billy Eckstine, Count Basie, and Nat King Cole. On the right, receipts and postcards recall the trip to Hawaii.

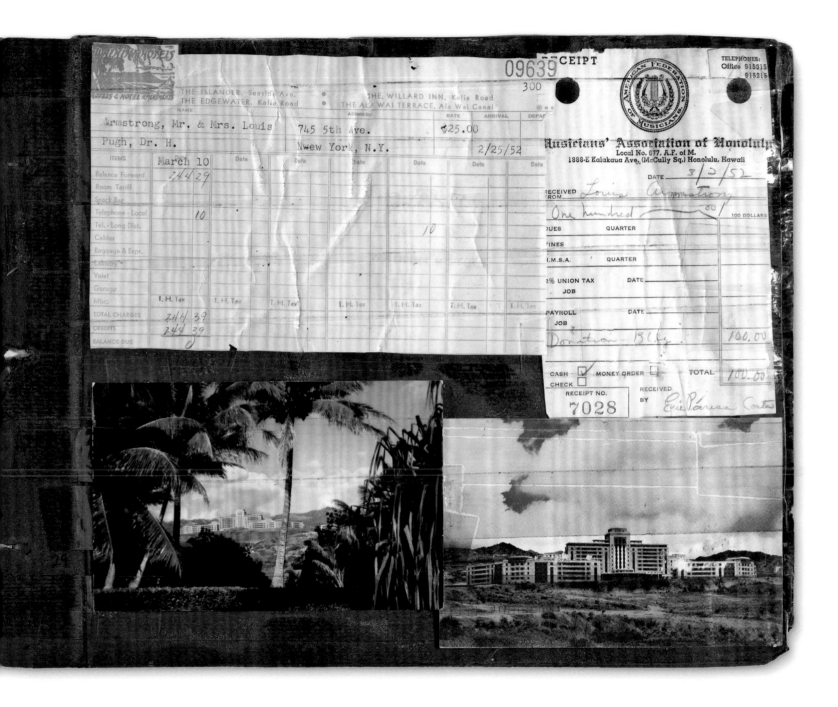

In this energetic spread, Armstrong employs color to good effect. On the left he shows other musicians in a "Dixieland" band, his own recording with the vocal group the Rhythmaires for an upcoming Bing Crosby television appearances, the popular 1950s singer Johnnie Ray, and on a more personal note, the retirement of Captain Joseph Jones, the head of the Municipal Boys' Home, formerly the Colored Waifs' Home, where Louis was placed from 1913 to 1914.

On the right-hand page Satchmo has provocative fun with the inflatable bra, an abstract of an article regarding Jane Russell's dress, and the placement of Martin and Lewis at the feet of actress Susan Hayward.

In this lively, incongruous scrapbook page, Satchmo records the dalliances of King Farouk of Egypt, perhaps purposefully placing him with those "million dollar" comedians Dean Martin and Jerry Lewis. He would appear with Jerry Lewis on the radio along with Bob Hope and Tallulah Bankhead, and with the comedy team on *The Colgate Comedy Hour.*

Louis maintains the incongruity on the opposite page, combining an ad for a jazz club in San Francisco and a greeting card from Lucille with a humorous article about a prison band in need of a clarinetist but "no rush is expected to fill the job."

On the left Louis celebrates
various stars of stage, screen,
and music. On the right he
continues his exposition of his
work on the film *Glory Alley*.

Singing in New Orleans bar in scene from *Glory Alley*, Louis Armstrong in role of Shadow Johnson, is joined on chorus by boxer Socks Barbaroso (Ralph Meeker), star of picture, and Gilbert Roland.

Hailing his pal Socks Barbaroso as new world's champion in scene from *Glory Alley*, Armstrong expresses his sentiments on trumpet as others drink to boxer's health. Seated at table is feminine lead Leslie Caron, pretty dancing sensation of *An American In Paris*. Jazz King Louis plays four solos in picture which is his eighth major movie.

Witness to dramatic incident, Armstrong watches as Kurt Kasznar, movie father to Leslie Caron, snaps cane in anger because daughter's boy friend, Meeker, is GI.

Wife Lucille

Performing for bar patrons, Armstrong sings to piano support of Pat Golden. He also introduces by song and trumpet the movie theme song, *Glory Alley*. His only wardrobe in film is casual attire of sport shirt and slacks, vest and straw hat.

Continued on Next Page

The extreme diagonal pushed
the music ahead, much like
Armstrong's playing.

Unidentified horn player, an
airline pilot, and Louis on
the move.

The missing piece creates a
ghostly form. Louis himself
looks surprised.

"Pops, it sure was the greatest thing that ever happened to me. Me and music got married at the home." —Louis Armstrong

In this superb collage, the base
of the Eiffel Tower holds up
the rest of the composition,
including a publicity photo from
The Five Pennies.

Satchmo's playing delights police
officers, sailors, and civilians alike.

A surprising use of found art,
Louis dubs the figures "Pops"
and "Lucille."

From the look on his face,
Louis told one of his many
off-color jokes.

A beautiful, serious portrait.

Character actor Allen Jenkins, known for playing tough guys and gangsters, whom Louis costarred with in *A Song Is Born*, 1948, is put to dramatic use here as well.

A wonderful all-type, modernist
collage makes the most of
printed matter.

On the right is Louis with Mrs. Stella
Oliver, wife of Joe "King" Oliver, taken in
New Orleans.

A tribute to feminine beauty featuring actress and dancer Leslie Caron. Louis playfully displays that he is an "active," "permanent," "honorary" member of the Leslie Caron fan club.

Louis keeps fans enthralled.

Handwritten song titles are combined with photomontage for a musical effect. There is no question that much care was taken with the composition, with the photos most likely considered first, as the type wraps around the photography. He uses a photograph of a marquee to add his name.

Compositionally, Louis made the most out of the existing box artwork and applied tape to create a rhythmic portrait of All-Star horn player Trummy Young. Young played with Armstrong for several years, and Armstrong knowingly chose the title "Fidelitone" in honor of his bandmate. Young once said that even though he played with Satchmo for so many years he still could be brought to tears by Louis's playing.

Left: A postcard from Acapulco from Louis's sister Beatrice, who signed it with her nickname, Mama. **Below:** As Louis says, this one "speaks for itself."

Not all of Louis's art was
personal, as is evidenced in this
exuberant nod to beach culture.

Louis gave this one away as a
present, no doubt because Lucille
would not have approved.

Louis was awarded the Jazz Music
Prize, instituted in 1939, in 1959
in France, and was declared an
Honorary President.

Great 33 1/3 rpm album art
echoes Louis's own designs.

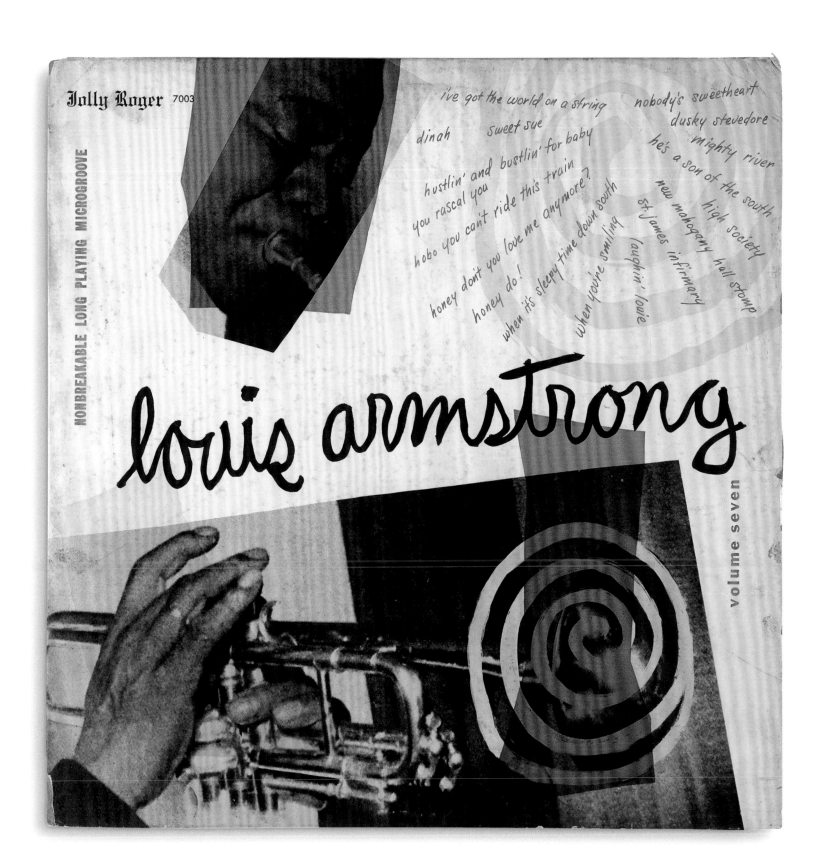

Jolly Roger 7003

NONBREAKABLE LONG PLAYING MICROGROOVE

i've got the world on a string

nobody's sweetheart

dusky stevedore

dinah   sweet sue

mighty river

he's a son of the south

hustlin' and bustlin' for baby

high society

you rascal you

hobo you can't ride this train

new mahogany hall stomp

honey don't you love me anymore?

st james infirmary

honey do!

when it's sleepy time down south

laughin' louie

when you're smiling

louis armstrong

volume seven

Below: A playful cover for Decca
Records. **Right:** His goodwill is
clearly evident.

DL 8488

LOUIS
AND
THE
ANGELS

with chorus
and orchestra
directed by
Sy Oliver

When Did You Leave Heaven?
You're A Heavenly Thing
I Married An Angel
A Sinner Kissed An Angel
Angela Mia
Angel Child
And The Angels Sing
Fools Rush In
I'll String Along With You
Angel
The Prisoner's Song
Goodnight Angel

DECCA
RECORDS
HIGH FIDELITY

Printed in U.S.A.

CL 840

COLUMBIA

A HIGH FIDELITY RECORDING
LP

European Concert Recordings by

AMBASSADOR SATCH

® "Columbia", Ⓖ Marcas Reg. Printed in U.S.A.

Louis posed with All-Star band members, trombonist Jack Teagarden, pianist Earl "Fatha" Hines, clarinetist Barney Bigard, and bassist Arvel Shaw.

On this lively back of the box, Louis commemorates various aspects of his life: performances, film sound tracks, and radio appearances; interviews; a hotel he stayed at; a restaurant; and, of course, Swiss Kriss. Note the energetic use of red tape for the border.

personality, his virtuoso horn playing, his features, which he utilized to comic effect, often his bulk, his likeability, his appetite, his generosity, and he had discovered the perfect medium in which to preserve his legacy.[63] As with his music, these collages explode with kinetic, syncopated vigor, creating rhythms before your eyes.[64] His collages were more than just scrap-booking—much, much more.

When Louis comes on, man, it's like the atomic bomb arriving, for PEACE! —*Joe Bushkin, piano player*

In 1950, Louis publicly celebrated his fiftieth birthday and was paid many tributes, although in reality he was forty-nine. In an article in *Flair* magazine, entitled "Satchmo by Tallu," written by actress and friend Tallulah Bankhead, she compared Armstrong to painter Stuart Davis and placed him in the pantheon of "high" art:

Hot Stillscape for Six Colors by Stuart Davis whose purpose is to express in painting the elements of rhythm, harmony and contrast that Louis Armstrong expresses in jazz . . . if Satchmo had never heard a high F, or if he couldn't sing a note, I would still dig him because he is an authentically great man embodying all the best instincts by which people should conduct their lives. The major difficulty in talking about Louis Armstrong is that the quality which sets him apart and above other artists in his field

is the indefinable quality of genius which people devoted to the critical function have spent centuries trying to analyze, whatever the medium—literature, dramaturgy, dance, music, painting—any of the communicative arts.

However, it seems to me that the essence of Louis is that he feels in his soul in ineffable tragedy of human existence and manages to communicate it to the aware, perceptive listener, which is, in that last analysis, the proper province of all art.

Later that year he agreed to a meeting with the Pope with Lucille, who was raised Catholic, telling his wife, "I'll make the Pope laugh." When Pius XII asked Louis if he had any children, Armstrong replied, "No . . . but we keep tryin'."

I'm a Baptist, a good friend of the Pope's and I always wear a Jewish star a friend gave me for good luck. —*Louis Armstrong*

The yearlong celebration continued when the U.S. State Department officially thanked him for a series of recordings he did, which the Voice of America (the official multimedia broadcasting service of the U.S. government), beamed to every part of the globe.

In 1951, Louis showed up in the musical comedy *Here Comes the Groom*, directed by Frank Capra, during an airplane jam session featuring star Bing Crosby with uncredited cameos by frequent Crosby costar Dorothy Lamour, singer Cass Daley, and comedian Frank Fontaine.

Louis captures the infectious
spirit of popular 1950s comedian
Jack Leonard.

The energy of the front is
carried over to the back of the
box. **Right:** "That Happy Feeling"
sums it all up.

That Happy Feeling

Louis's life experiences and wide-ranging interests intersect on this box cover—the music of Tchaikovsky, Duke Ellington, and a tour of South America. The dashed line connects his notation of the tour with a snapshot most likely from that same tour.

Louis creates a deconstructivist
composition, employing white
medical tape. At bottom is a still
from *The Five Pennies*.

Louis moves our eye around the
art, utilizing white tape over
this photo of him chatting with
Paloma Efrom.

Bing Crosby, Frank Sinatra, and
Grace Kelly kick up their heels
as Satchmo provides the tune on
the set of *High Society*, 1956.

Such was Armstrong's level of fame that Crosby simply had to exclaim "The mighty Louie!" as he appeared, with no further introduction required, as Armstrong adds his vocal to "Misto Cristofo Columbo."

That same year he was interviewed by pioneering broadcast newsman Edward R. Murrow on his *See It Now* television program. Murrow was enthralled:

 Murrow: Now, what is a cat?

 Armstrong: Cat? A cat can be anybody from the guy in the gutter to a lawyer, doctor, the biggest man and the lowest man, but if he's in there with a good heart and enjoyin' the same music together, he's a cat.

 Murrow: Well, you know, listening to you tonight, I think I became a cat for the first time.[65]

A few years later Murrow took this show, added footage of Armstrong's world tours, and produced and narrated the feature film *Satchmo the Great*. Included in the documentary is a performance of "St. Louis Blues" that teams Armstrong and his All-Stars with Leonard Bernstein and a symphony orchestra, as well as pen-and-ink illustrations of Louis's early years by renowned artist Ben Shahn, which were later reproduced in *Nugget* magazine, in 1957.[66]

It was reported in the *New York Post* on November 13, 1951, under the headline "The Egyptians Insist Louis Armstrong's A Spy": "In Egypt, they're making Louis Armstrong out to be a leader of an Israeli spy network. . . . He commented 'It's all Greek to me . . . Why don't you tell these people who are spreading this stuff to come around, I'll tell them a few good traveling salesman jokes.'"

As "Ambassador Satch" of both jazz and goodwill, he returned to tour Europe with his latest version of the All-Stars in 1952. Beginning with its February 22,

1952, issue, *Down Beat* began a series of comic strips based on Louis's life by J. Lee Anderson.

In 1954 he published his second autobiography, *Satchmo: My Life in New Orleans*. It was translated into several languages, including French and Norwegian. Unlike the first, *Swing That Music*, which was heavily ghosted, Armstrong's colorful and idiosyncratic voice comes though loud and clear. Following the success of this memoir, Louis began a third autobiography, tentatively titled *Gage*, a celebration of his Chicago years and of marijuana. When he gave the pages to his manager, Glaser destroyed them, fearing scandal. Those around Louis who censored him throughout the years misunderstood his gifts and creativity, fearing his unorthodoxy.[67]

In the biopic of Glenn Miller, released in 1953, starring James Stewart, Louis shows up for only one song, "Basin Street Blues," playing at "Connie's" in Harlem, fifty-two years old and playing himself at twenty-eight. As usual he gives his best, albeit a somewhat subdued performance in an overly subdued film, despite some distracting colored gel effects, supposedly to give the scene authenticity. When June Allyson, as Helen Berger Miller, asks "Who's that?" Miller (Stewart) responds incredulously, "Why, that's Louie Armstrong!"

On the popular television show *You Are There* Louis portrayed his hero King Oliver, in an episode entitled "The Emergence of Jazz," in 1954.

With the All-Stars in 1956, Armstrong toured Ghana, at the time known as the Gold Coast. In Accra, there were one hundred thousand in attendance, and in Léopoldville (now called Kinshasa), tribesmen painted themselves ochre and violet and carried him into the city stadium on a canvas throne.[68]

By year's end, Louis was performing in London at a benefit concert at the Royal Festival Hall for Hungarian refugees, accompanied by the Royal Philharmonic Orchestra. With a headline that boasted: "Satchmo Buries Liszt As London Cats

Roar" by United Press staff writer Robert Musel, the article described how the musical conductor, dismayed at the audience's raucous reaction to Armstrong's playing, stormed off the stage. "A packed audience of high-brows and jazz fans—the mink and blue jeans set—created such an uproar that the conductor Norman Del Mar gave up any attempt to complete the classical part of the program. He stalked off. . . . The trouble started when Mr. Del Mar underestimated Satchmo's great lung power. . . . After each number the crew-cut college crowd and the rock 'n' rollers roared their approval. The mink-and-tails set joined in and soon the joint was jumping."

During this decade Louis would have two major hits, "Blueberry Hill," recorded before Fats Domino's version, and "Mack the Knife," before Bobby Darin's.

While playing a concert in Knoxville, Tennessee, in February before a segregated audience of two thousand whites and one thousand blacks, a stick of dynamite was tossed at the theater. Fortunately no one was injured in the explosion. Louis quipped, "That's all right, folks, it's just the phone."[69]

In yet another outing with Bing Crosby in 1956's *High Society*, Louis appeared Puck-like, not only narrating the story but also driving the action forward. Perhaps his role seemed somewhat familiar to him as Louis had appeared as Bottom in *Swingin' the Dream*, an all-black adaptation of Shakespeare's *A Midsummer Night's Dream*, on Broadway in 1939. Butterfly McQueen played Puck.[70]

In a song written especially for him by Cole Porter, he opened *High Society* with a prologue, playing himself once again, singing "High Society Calypso" from the back of his tour bus sporting a jaunty porkpie hat, laying out the tale of Dexter (Crosby) who "is nursing the blues" because his ex-wife is about to remarry "a square." Based on *Philadelphia Story*, Armstrong sings:

But, Brother Dexter,
just trust your Satch,
to stop that weddin' and
kill that match.
I'll not toot my trumpet to
start the fun,
and play in such a way that
she'll come back to you, son,

In High, High So-,
High So-ci,
High So-ci-ety.

Armstrong ends with a scat and adds, "Can you dig ol' Satchmo swinging in the beautiful high society?" and announces "end of song, beginning of story." Dexter greets him with "Hey, Pops, how's the chops? Man, you've been all over Europe since I seen you last. Been to Sweden? Skoll!"

Armstrong reappears midway through for a jam session that causes Tracy (Grace Kelly) to come over to complain, thus bringing Dexter and her together. Satch plays another song, casting a spell over Dexter, furthering the story gleefully. "Now we're getting warm!" he duets with Crosby on a rousing "Now You Has Jazz" and closes out the film, New Orleans–style, by proclaiming "End of story!"

 Even though I've played with a lot of them—Danny Kaye, Sinatra—I don't even know where they live. In fact I've never been invited to the home of a movie star, not even Bing's.

—Louis Armstrong[71]

The following year Louis appeared on *The Edsel Show* in a spirited performance with Frank Sinatra.

Sinatra: Professor A?

Armstrong: Yes, Professor S?

Sinatra can barely contain himself and his appreciation of Satchmo is palpable.

In September of 1957, Armstrong and the All-Stars were set to tour Russia in a U.S. government sponsored tour. A young writer from the North Dakota paper, the *Grand Forks Herald*, Larry Lubenow interviewed Louis in his hotel room.[72] Toward the end of the interview the reporter asked Louis his reaction to the news that black high school students had been prevented from attending Central High School in Little Rock, Arkansas. Arkansas governor Orval Faubus had ordered the Arkansas National Guard to prevent the nine students from entering the high school and President Dwight Eisenhower hesitated in taking action. Uncharacteristically Louis responded, "The way they are treating people in the South, the government can go to hell! It's getting so bad a colored man doesn't have any country." He went on to state that President Eisenhower was "two faced" and "has no guts." He was quoted as calling Faubus an "uneducated plowboy," although his actual language was much more colorful, a two-word four-syllable expletive deleted. He promptly announced he was canceling the overseas tour.

The news was carried in all the major outlets and Armstrong found himself embroiled in controversy from all sides. He was criticized by whites for insulting the president. Syndicated columnist Jim Bishop wrote, "I checked the newspaper files to see what Armstrong had done for the people of his race. I haven't found anything."[73]

At the same time Sammy Davis, Jr. quickly gave an interview declaring, "Louis Armstrong doesn't speak for us," criticizing Armstrong for not speaking out sooner. Ironically, years later Davis himself would be criticized for the infamous photograph of him hugging Nixon at the height of Watergate and the Vietnam War.

What was unknown, however, was that Armstrong was a major financial supporter of Dr. Martin Luther King, Jr. and other civil rights activists. He simply chose not to mix politics with entertainment, at least until 1957. As a result of this notoriety the FBI accused him of being a communist and began keeping a file.

A note's a note in any language.
—*Louis Armstrong*

Then came the movie *The Five Pennies*, in 1959, a biopic of trumpeter Red Nichols. Danny Kaye played Nichols onscreen, and it was falsely rumored that Armstrong played the cornet parts—which in fact were played by Nichols himself. Louis received third billing, right after Kaye and Barbara Bel Geddes. The film begins in 1924. Nichols, fresh from Ogden, Utah, wants to go see Louis play. "There's a new trumpet player up in Harlem, he just came from New Orleans. The boys told me he's just great. They're going up to listen to him tonight, and I thought I would go up." Up at the nightclub, after some high jinks, the club darkens to reveal the bell of a horn on stage, revealing a mature Louis once again playing his youthful self, blowing and sweating, playing a chorus of "After You're Gone." "Next to my father that's the greatest trumpet playing I've ever heard in my whole life," exclaims Red (Kaye). During a rousing "(Won't You Come Home) Bill Bailey," Red challenges him to a duet, but then gets sick from the speakeasy "tea" he's imbibed.

GRAND HOTEL
ROMA

It is clear in this letter to Dizzy Gillespie and his wife, Lorraine, that any old differences had long been resolved, and they enjoyed a warm friendship.

July, 1st, 1959.

Dear Dizzy and Lorraine:

Thanks for the lovely wire.. But there's 'onething that you both should always remember—you can't kill a nigger...Ha Ha Ha.... Ole Sidney Bachet—and Big Sid Catlett, were trying to get me to come up there with them and hold that 1st, chair down on the trumpet... Probably they would have had a little luck if they were'nt so damn cheap. Huh – they only wanted to pay me Union Scales...Shit. I got more then that when I first came up North from down in Galilee... Tee Hee... So I blinded them with (G)......

We will probably beat this letter home...We are leaving today from Rome... Lucille Dr Schiff(Ah' livin (G)perin – My Nurse Doctuh Pugh – A Countess (filthy rich)—and the Nurse' husband; we all spent our last night with Brick Top... Good Ole Brick, We all took turns (Hmm turns) in doin a number.... I'm back at myself...Ole Doc Schiff put some kind of jive into me, that's making eveything stand up..Better than before...Wow. So long for now..

Your Boy, Ol, Dush....

Louis Armstrong

Mr and Mrs Dizzy Gellespie.
34-68 – 106 Street
Corona, New York.
U S A

Dizzy Gillespie, Jackie Gleason,
Louis Armstrong During Rehearsal
of TIMEX ALL STAR JAZZ TV SHOW

Associated Booking Corp.
JOE GLASER, President
New York, Chicago, Hollywood

I made A Bee line, over to the Paramount and
Ol Bing Crosby AS, WE "CATS' UP'IN' HARLEM' Called
him in those days.— Ofcourse nowadays, I Call's him
Pappa Bing.— The show I Caught at
the Paramount, was A thrill as well as
A surprise to me. He had Matured Wonderfuly.
And Above All, A very fine Comedian. my my.
that Man, delivered, A Couple of lines while singing
BING
to A Chick,—made me laugh so hard and so loud,
until my Stomach was hurting And I had to
hold it.— The whole House Just Roared.
MR TUMMY
He layed one of his Cute gags on her.
GAGS
And the Chick he was singing to, had a real
hard time keeping A straight face.
In 1930 I went out to California to join
the band which was playing at Frank
Sebastian's Cotton Club.—Bing and his
Trio IN'CULVER'CITY'CALIF. were really Romping

Left: Louis and Bing Crosby enjoyed mutual respect and admiration throughout the years, and here Louis describes how Crosby had "matured wonderfully." **Below:** From one of Louis' binders: Satchmo and Der Bingle blast out "Now You Has Jazz" on the set of the 1956 film *High Society*.

Armstrong notes, "You look a little shaky there, son, you better sit this one out. We'll get to the volunteers later." Red manages to rally and plays a duet with Satchmo on "Battle Hymn of the Republic," to enthusiastic applause. Midway through the film Red takes his eight-year-old daughter to see "Louie" and we are treated to an extreme close-up of Louis singing (beautifully) "Good Night, Sleep Tight." Louis and Red sing "When the Saints Going Marching In" with new "hip" lyrics,

Red: What about Chopin?

Satchmo: Solid man!

Next Kaye does a comic impression of Armstrong. "Look at this cat diggin' me, face and all!" As usual Louis pushes his costar higher and higher, and what could have been mundane shtick becomes the musical highlight of the film. "There was Bix, there was Louie and there was me," Nichols hyperbolizes. The film ends with Red's comeback at a club after a seven-year layoff, Louis leading the march of musicians in the club to surprise Red and save the day.

In 1959 he returned with the All-Stars for another tour of Europe. The turnout and the reviews were extremely positive; the *New York Post* reported on February 9, 1959: "Satchmo a Berlin Sellout." In March they performed at a standing-room-only crowd at the Gaumont State Theatre in London. In June it was reported that in Geneva dozens of teenage fans were "Besieged by the music, the youths broke lose and besieged Armstrong at the end of the show." The following month the *Toronto Star*, dated Thursday April 2, 1959, ran the

headline: "Satchmo Jams 'Em: Yugoslavs Sit Hours to Applaud Jazz" and under it: " The show was scheduled to start at 9 p.m., but the concert hall was packed three hours earlier. The fans were informed that the plane bringing Armstrong and his six-man combo from Austria was behind time. . . . Shortly before midnight, Armstrong and his band appeared on the stage. . . . It was after 2 a.m. when the session ended. The musicians received a standing ovation from the happy fans."

Music is a common denominator. Jazz fans are the same all over the world. —*Louis Armstrong*

On June 25, newspapers throughout the world reported that Satchmo was hospitalized in Spoleto, Italy. That day the *New York Post* ran the headline "Satchmo Goes Into Coma: Rome Heart Doctors Called." The extent and cause of his illness were contradicted in the press, and reports were filed on a daily basis: "'Satchmo' has made a strong recovery, Spoleto (Italy), June 26. "Armstrong sat up in bed today, moved his fingers as if playing a trumpet and hummed 'Sunny Side of the Street.'" The *New York Post*, June 29, 1959: "Satchmo Quits Hospital—He's Fully Recovered."

The doctors disagree whether it was pneumonia or a heart attack. Louis downplayed the whole affair.

They called it pneumonia, I just ate too much. —*Louis Armstrong*

1960s and Beyond . . .

What A Wonderful World

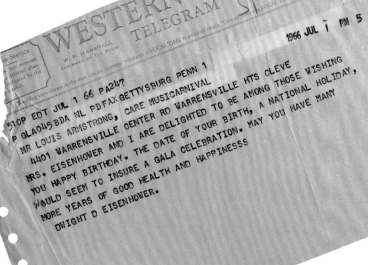

As a young child Louis's mother made him take a "physic" every day, in the commonly held belief that a laxative protected against illness. Louis continued this practice throughout his life. The brand he utilized initially was Pluto Water, and he was such an advocate that he would sign with correspondence "Am Pluto Waterly yours." He believed in its healing power just as he believed in the healing power of music.[74] He then discovered the herbal laxative Swiss Kriss and quickly became their spokesman, extolling the virtues to anyone who would listen, including members of the British royal family. He posed on a toilet seat with his pants at his knees for an advertisement with the tagline: "Satch says, 'Leave it all behind ya!'" and sent the same photo out as a Christmas card. He began signing letters "Swiss Krissly yours." He loved food and his weight went up and down the scale like his playing; one need only watch his film and television appearances to appreciate how often. His love of food combined with his fond remembrance of his beloved mother, and he also regularly signed his letters: "Am red beans and ricely yours." He created his own diet, "Lose Weight the Satchmo Way."

Be sharp, feel sharp, stay sharp.

—Louis Armstrong

Louis returned with the All-Stars to Africa. It was announced that half the profits from his tour in November would go to Nyatsime College, near Salisbury in Southern Rhodesia (now Zimbabwe). On November 7, 1960, *The New York Times* ran the following: "A Horn Wins Nairobi, Too: Kenyans Say 'We Dig You, "Satch" in Praise of Jazz Band's African Tour."

On *The Dinah Shore Chevy Show* in 1961, Louis performed "Gabriel's Horn," his performance was right up there with his earliest exuberant ones as it came to a rollicking halt, almost collapsing under its own power.

In March of 1962, Leonard Feather, prominent jazz critic and longtime friend, wrote an article for *Down Beat* that declared "Dear Virginia. Yes, there is a Satchmo." Going on to state that "Louis had no eyes to become a politician, he is by nature, a thorough diplomat."[75]

Throughout the decade he toured internationally: Africa, Australia, Czechoslovakia, Formosa, France, East and West Germany, Great Britain, Hong Kong, Hungary, Iceland, India, Japan, Korea, Mexico, the Netherlands, New Zealand, Romania, Singapore, Scandinavia, and Yugoslavia. In 1961, Velma Middleton, the rotund singer

Best wishes To Dr Schiff

Louis Armstrong

Satchmo

By Lucille Armstrong
Louis Armstrong

Lose Weight
The "Satchmo" Way

featuring

Swiss Kriss....herbal laxative
Bisma Rex....it cuts gas
Fresh orange juice....it's
   delicious, softens fat.

You can buy it in any drug store....
Rexall Drug Store

Directions

At Bedtime

P. S. Your first dose will be real heavy, in order to start blasting right away, and get the ball to rolling. After you get over your surprises and whatnots, you'll be very happy. The first week, take a tablespoonful of <u>Swiss Kriss</u>. Put it into your mouth and rinse it down with a glass of water. Fifteen minutes later, drink a large glass of orange juice. Don't eat no food before going to bed. After the first week, cut <u>Swiss Kriss</u> down to a teaspoonful every night.

At Breakfast Time

Large glass of orange juice and black coffee or tea, etc......

At Lunch Time

Eat whatever you want....as much as you want....just have slices of tomatoes with lemon juice over it....mmm, it's good. In fact, you may choose any salad that you like....just see that you have <u>some kind</u>, any kind. Coffee, tea, or, etc. Twenty minutes later, <u>take</u> a tablespoonful of Bisma Rex. Stir it in a glass of water....stir real good....and drink it right on down. Chase it down with a half glass of water.

Between Meals

If you should get a little hungry between meals, just drink a large glass of orange juice, two glasses if you should desire.

Supper Time

You can eat from soup to nuts....eat as much as you want to. Please see that you have, at least, either sliced tomatoes (with lemon juice) or your favorite salad. All kinds of <u>greens</u> are good for the stomach. So....eat to your satisfaction. Of course, the less you eat is in

An intriguing, unexpected
overhead shot of Louis doing one
of the things he likes best.

who had been with the All-Stars since the late 1940s, died while on tour in Sierra Leone.

In 1964, Louis recorded "Hello, Dolly!" from the Broadway show of the same name, transforming the song as he had done so many times before, turning it into his own. It became a number-one hit, knocking the Beatles' "Do You Want to Know a Secret" off the top of the charts and introducing Louis to yet another generation. This record should end once and for all the incorrect pronunciation of his name: "Hello, Dolly, this is Louis, Dolly," but people insist on calling him "Louie," perhaps because he was perceived as such a warm and humble figure that he would never be so formal. Five years later he performed the song in the film version, starring Barbra Streisand, and as he often did throughout his career, he stole the show.

Alongside the Beatles and others of the British Invasion, Louis appeared performing this song on *The Ed Sullivan Show*, watched weekly by millions. In his younger days the twinkle in his eye was born of mischievousness and youthful vigor. The joy he conveyed was just as subversive as it was enchanting. Now, as an older man, the very same twinkle was viewed by the boomer generation as that of a kindly old nonthreatening gentleman. The nickname he applied to everyone else as well, unbeknownst to his new audience, summed it all up when applied to him: "Pops." The white handkerchief, once his trademark, was simply there to serve the purpose

of mopping up his profuse perspiration. The riffs he played were Dixieland, and few realized he was one of the legendary driving forces of that sound. By this time he had honed his playing to a modernist "less is more" simplification, riffing with fewer notes, boiling down his whole New Orleans experience into a single solo, the act of a mature artist. But those who weren't cognizant of all that had gone before missed the point. Had his marijuana consumption been more well known, there is no doubt Louis would have reached folk hero status with the younger generation within in few scant years. As it was, they viewed him as a lovable grandfatherly figure. In 1968 he recorded Disney *Songs the Satchmo Way*, introducing himself to an even younger generation.

In December of 1965 there was a tribute at Carnegie Hall, for his contributions to a youth fund program and his fifty years in show business.

He returned to New Orleans, for the first time in many years, after passage of the Civil Rights Act. He had boycotted his hometown because of segragation, and performed there with an integrated band in the city's Jazz Museum.

Louis's next to-last big screen appearance arrived with the release of *A Man Called Adam*, directed by Leo Penn in 1966. His most dramatic role ever, Armstrong received second billing after star Sammy Davis Jr., but above Ossie Davis and

DAILY NEWS, THURSDAY, DECEMBER 18, 1969

"Hello, Dolly!' Is a Super Musical

By WANDA HALE

★ ★ ★ ★

Barbra Streisand

Louis with Barbra Streisand, from the
film version of *Hello, Dolly!*, five years
after his top-ten hit.

Louis forms his own musical quartet.

MAESTRO
RECORDING TAPE
Made in U.S.

Left: Louis and Lucille.

An older Lucille and Louis
peer out as floating heads
loom overhead.

A playful collage featuring actress Lauren Bacall and the title "Satchmo Plays King Oliver," one of his albums, on which Louis plays the music of his hero, King Oliver. Note that Louis creates the form of a hand with his scissors rather than conforming to the contour of the photo on the unidentified man.

Louis practices before playing
with the New York Philharmonic,
conducted by Leonard Bernstein.

"What he does is real, and true, and honest, and simple, and even noble. Every time this man puts his trumpet to his lips, even if only to practice three notes, he does it with his whole soul."—*Leonard Bernstein*

Louis Armstrong tunes up for concert with New York Philharmonic in 1956. Leonard Bernstein conducted.

The Armstrongs party with the
Basies in 1969.

Louis and Lucille meet with Pope
Pius XII in 1968.

Louis's wife was Catholic. In the
inset Louis talks on the radio.

Religious imagery punctuates this
late collage . . .

. . . and religious text decorates
the verso in the manner of an
illuminated manuscript.

MERRY CHRISTMAS AND A HAPPY NEW YEAR

from our album of greetings

LUCILLE AND LOUIS ARMSTRONG

Holiday Greetings

Louis & Lucille Armstrong

Telegram

643P EDT JUL 3 69 SYA284
SY NB271 TLX WHC0 19) GOV PD TEMPOARY WHITEHOUSE KEY BISCAYNE
FLA 3 606P EDT

LOUIS ARMSTRONG, REPORT DELIVERY
3456 107 ST CORONA NY

MRS. NIXON I JOIN IN HEARTFELT GOOD WISHES TO YOU O YOUR 69TH
BIRTHDAY. SOMEHOW IT IS MOST APPROTIATE THAT YOUR BIRTHDAY
SHOULD FALL ON THE FOURTH OF JULY, FOR FEW MWEN HAVE GIVEN
MORE THAN YOU TO OUR CULTURAL LORE, AND TO THE CREATION OF
INTERNATIONAL FRIENDSHIP ANDGOODWILL. WE WERE SORRY TO HEAR
R OF YOUR ILLNES, AAND WE HOPE THAT YOUR BIRTHDAY FINDS YOU
IN BETTER SPIRITS AND WELL ON THE ROAD TO RECOVERY. I KNOW
THAT A GRATEFUL NATION JOINS US IN APPLAUDING YOUR TALENT,
HUMOR, COMPAWSION AND UNIQUE, ENDURING CONTRIBUTION TO THE
AMERICAN HERITAGE. WE WISH YOU THE HAPPIEST OF BIRTHDAYS AND
A YEAR ENRICHED BY THE CONTENTMENT THAT DERIVES FROM HAVING

SF-1201 (R5-69)

Telegram

BROUGHT SO MUCH JOY AND GLADNESS TO YOUR FELLOWMAN
RICHARD NIXON
(640).

Telegram

1014P EDT JUL 4 69 SYA281 LA238
L LLH034 WK PDF LOS ANGELES CALIF 4 650P PDT

LOUIS ARMSTRONG, DLY 75
34-56 107 CORONA NY

HAPPY BIRTHDAY, POPS. LOVE TO LUCILLE
MARIE BRAYNT

Satchmo goes country and western, in perhaps his most eccentric musical outing, although he recorded with "The Singing Brakeman" Jimmy Rodgers in 1930. Next page: Louis records in longhand his experiences in his neighborhood in Corona, Queens. It was unprecedented for an international celebrity to reside in such humble surroundings, and there is no question it was by design rather than necessity—he and Lucille easily could have chosen an estate on Long Island or a Malibu mansion. Indeed, Louis loved to swim and no doubt would have enjoyed a swimming pool.

Rather, Louis took delight in his neighbors and celebrates them in this charming autobiographical sketch. He was, once and always, a man of the people.

Louis discusses his protracted illness in this memoir from 1969, stating that he hadn't played horn in "almost three years," but that he is on the eve of returning to performing.

In the "Spanish barbershop" he grooved on music from south of the border, and borrowed the records to take home and record on his reel-to-reel. "They all know that I personally love all kinds of music from all nationalities. And that ain't no lie."

Barber Shops

In my neighbood where I live in Corona.
I have (2) Barber shops. I can get my
Hair when ever I want to. The Soul
Barber shop closes on ~~Sundays~~ Mondays rain
or shine. My Spanishes Barber shop
never closes, except, only on Sundays.
Sometimes, if I just have a Hair cut
on a monday, And just can't wait
until the next day, I will make a
bee line to the Spanish one, And they
are just as glad to have me, anyway.
It's just ~~just~~ that I'll give ole Soulee
the Benefit of the doubt Anyway.
And we Soulees speak the same
Languages,— S languages— the usual
B.S.— talk Loud— etc. And they both
Just Knock me out.   (more)

2

And what's so nice about the whole thing
even those spanish barbers, they are
all from the Old Countries (their Countries)
their Countries somewhere in this world.
And they all remembered me when I was
touring all over the world - blowing my
little trumpet - singing and entertaining
them, which they're very happy to remind
me of it. Just think - since those days.
They all (most of them) have married
and have big families, and have
instilled in their Children's mind how
how they enjoyed Louis Satchmo Armstrong's
music. And their kids, should do the
same. I see the warmpth, the Foreigners
gave to me - the same as my soul
Brothers. When I approach them. doing
my Travels, all down in South America,

(more)

3 I received the same feeling. And I have'nt played the Horn for ages. Especially since I have been Ill for almost three years. But now – gradually I am begining to Blow my Horn + and sing and Make Quite a few Phublic Appearances again. Which is making Everybody Very happy including my little ole self. Speaking of this little Spanish barber Shop, they had a whole Rack of the Spanish Albums, which they keep in a Corner of the shop. They were recorded down in Miami Florida and are on Sale for Anybody who would like to by One. They'r Recorded by the finest Spanish Singers there is. The price is (90¢) for each Album. Sitting right next to me in this shop Waiting to get his hair Cut also – he and I stuck up a Conversation about music and Records etc – And I told him about my love for Spanish music and

(more)

4

And asked him to do me a favor and
pick out one of those albums for me
especially the one that he enjoyed listning
to the most, of he was very happy to
do that for me. He picked the Album
which was recorded by- LOS EXITOS DE
ARMANDO. A real beautiful one. And
that can really sing good. As soon as
the finished cutting my hair - I went
reight straight home (my house) which
was Just around the Corner from the
Barber shop - And recorded the whole
Album on my big Tape Recorder.
Gave it an Index number + everything.
of, yes, the Album was was Recorded in
Florida by a Company named TAPE.
This kid was a Teenage Boy who the
name of Louis Armstrong for many years.
I even told him - About the times, during my
Traveling all over the world for (54) years
and every Country that I Visited - there
was always Some big Record Star who

(more)

5

came up to me & gave one of their personal Albums to take back to America and record it into my files. Because they all Know that I personally love's all Kinds of Music from all Nationalities. And that Ain't No lie. I shall always remember that particular evening in that Barber Shop.

Below: Arthur Godfrey, Dina Merril, and New York Governor Nelson Rockefeller celebrate Louis. **Right:** "We Have All the Time in the World." Louis writes out song lyrics in longhand, perhaps for a recording date or performance, but in many ways these seem to sum up his philosophy. **Overleafs:** "Uncle" Louis and "Aunt" Lucille were a vital part of the neighborhood, watching several generations come and go. When Louis fell ill and was home recuperating, they would remain quiet, and when he was on the mend and playing horn once again, they would call out of concern if he did not play. Louis was very proud of his home, which sported "a bathroom with mirrors everywhere, since we are disciples to laxatives." He described a visit to the local Chinese restaurant, where he became so involved in signing autographs for the local kids that he didn't eat his meal. His fortune cookie predicted: "Social pleasure and a most fortunate future."

We have all the time in the world.

We have all the time in the world —
Time enough for life to unfold —
All the precious things love has in store —
We have all the love in the world —
If that's all we have you'll find —
We need nothing more —
Every step of the way will find us —
With the cares of the world —
Far behind us —
We have all the time in the world —
Just for love — —
Nothing more — nothing less —
Only love.

Only Love

1

Our Neiborhood

When My wife Lucille + I Moved into
this Neighborhood there were Mostly white
people. A few Colored families. Just think —
through the (29) years that we've been
living in this house, we have seen
Just About (3) generations Come up
On this Perticular Block - 107 street
between 34th, + 37th Ave. Lots of them
have grown up — Married had Children.
Their Children + they still Come And
Visit — Aunt Lucille + Uncle Louis.
And there's, Death in our block
Lucille Always a Bake a Turkey —
Ham, etc put it in a big basket
And take it over to the house — so
the people who Come And sit up with
the Decease will have Sandwiches
Coffee, etc. Recently (8) people

(more)

2

has died since Louis Armstrong came out
of the Hospital. Even the new Neighbors
get to knows us. And we Respect each
other greatly. When (Pops) was sick
And just out of the Hospital – Nobody
bothered him and kept very Quiet so
that he would he would be disturbed.
Now that has recuperated – feel good –
blowing — HIS HORN — every evening before supper
with his doctor's permission, the whole
Neighhood rejoice at hearing his
horn everyday. And when (Pops) miss
blowing his horn, a couple of days
the Neighbors will Call on the
phone saying, is (Pops) O K? –
we haven't heard his horn for
A few days. Is there Anything wrong?
Then Lucille will tell them, No
(more)

3

Pops is alright. He's, just been busy doing other things, such a Interviews in his Den for his Fans - All over the world. which them very much. Thats why Lucille + Pops feel that we should move. We don't think that we Could be more relaxed And have better Neighbors any place else. So we stay put. After all - we have a very lovely home. The house may not be nicest looking front. But when one Visit the Interior of the Armstrong's home, they, see a whole lot of Comfort happiness + the nicest things. Such as that wall to wall Bed - A Bath Room with mirrors Everywhere. Since we Are Deciples to Laxatives. A Garage with a Magic Gate up + down to it. And ofcourse our Birthmark Car, A Cadillac! (yea)

(more)

4

The kids in our block just thrill when they see our garage gate up, And our fine Cadillac ooze on out. They just rejoice And say, Hi Louis + Lucille – Your Car is so beautiful Coming out of that raise up gate. which knocks me out. There's, a Chinees Restaurant in Corona where Lucille + I have our Chinees Food when we're in the mood. While sitting there in the Restaurant waiting for out food to be Served, And by the time our food is being Served – the kids of the Neighborhood might pass by And look through the window And see Satchmo And Round up All the kids in the neighborhood that satchmo + Lucille

(more)

5

is sitting in the Restaurant, And
the whole Neighborhood of kids Come
And As soon As the waiter bring our
food, All these kids make a bee line in
the Restaurant to my table for Autographs.
See — I still have'nt eaten my food
for Autographing for the kids. The
funny thing About it All — they all must
have their Names on their Autographs.
It by the time I finished, hmm
my food were very Cold. So
I Ate My Fortune Cookies, which
read — One read A SOCIAL PLEASURE AND)
MOST FORTUNATE FUTURE)
The other Fortune Cookie said —
YOUR ROMANCE WILL BE A LONG AND
LASTING ONE. So we left the
Wagon Seed And when we went home
Lucille fixed me a beeg Dagwood
(more) Sandwhich

6

At home where we live in Corona is so lively — We have two dogs. They are Male + Female. And Snorers; they Are two very fine watch dogs. They not only Bark when the door bell rings, but anybody who comes' up our steps, they Bark their (A)spirin off, The Male Dog who is the older one, his name is "TRUMPET" The Female, the baby, her name is TRINKET — I gave Trumpet to Lucille And Mr Joe Glaser gave us Trinket. And when the two of them start Barking together — Oh Boy what a Duet,

An aging Louis takes flight with
All-Star Tyree Glenn.

Cicely Tyson, who both had much more screen time. It was an extremely bleak yet powerful film, and Louis portrayed Willie "Sweet Daddy" Ferguson, an elderly jazz musician whose time in the spotlight had come and gone, who stood in contrast to the popular but troubled cornet player Adam Johnson (Davis) and also to Louis's recent real success.

There is one telling bit of dialogue during a party scene midway through:

> **Willie:** I reckon an old man makes these kids uneasy. Seem like the people don't know what to say to me.
> **Adam:** Maybe it's that they just don't know what to say to a genius.

The film tackles some serious issues, including drug addiction, although not directly mentioned, and civil rights. Tyson plays an activist from the South who spent time in jail, and there is a volatile tour of the southern states that ends in violence. Despite his costar billing, evidence of his star status even at this late date, Louis is mostly employed as support to the main characters, portrayed by Davis and Tyson. As such he does a credible

and affable job as an elder statesman, who appears on the surface at ease but is melancholic just beneath. One is left to wonder, had times been different and were Louis offered more dramatic roles such as this, what would his acting portfolio have been like? Perhaps, like Frank Sinatra, whose son appears in the film, he would have starred in a wider range of roles, and it would have added more breadth to his overall oeuvre.

In 1968 Armstrong suffered shortness of breath and his doctors ordered him to the hospital. Instead, Louis disappeared for two weeks, spending time up in Harlem, visiting friends. Meanwhile his condition worsened and he was forced to go to Beth Israel Medical Center in Manhattan, suffering heart and kidney problems. He discovered his manager Joe Glaser was in the same hospital, comatose, and Glaser died shortly afterward. While hospitalized, Louis penned, in longhand, an affectionate memoir to the Karnofsky family of his New Orleans youth, and lovingly dedicated it to Glaser, "The best friend I ever had. May the lord bless him, watch over him always"[76]

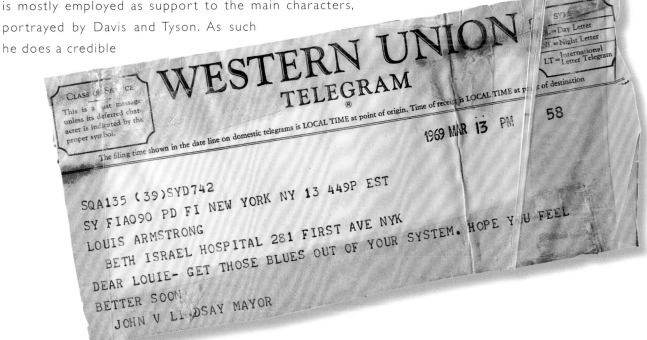

Louis and Lucille with one of the
co-composers of "Blueberry Hill,"
possibly Vincent Rose; the song
was a major hit for Armstrong
in 1952.

Louis and his manager and
friend Joe Glaser.

Satchmo sports a cigarette
holder in this collage with
Joe Glaser.

Louis honors the memory of Joe
Glaser shortly after his passing.

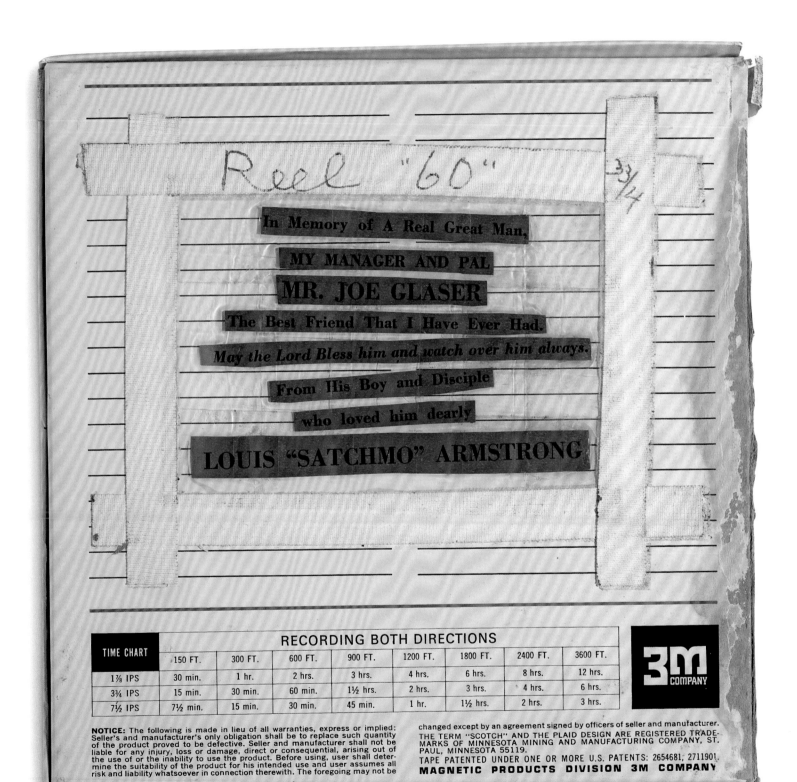

Upon his return from the hospital Louis created these last two collages. He died a few days later, on July 6, 1971.

in Heaven will have to wait for old Louis,'

THE MIAMI HERALD June 25, 1971

Satchmo Bouncing Back, Eager to Work Again

Trumpeter Louis Armstrong at Practice
...shows off his recovery from near-fatal illness

That same year Louis started the Louis Armstrong Educational Foundation, which has benefited school-children ever since.

Louis remained in the hospital for several months. In May he returned to the recording studio to record the album *With Friends*, the roster of musicians including Eddie Condon, Miles Davis, Ornette Coleman, and Bobby Hackett, singing only, on doctor's orders. The following summer Louis performed at the Newport Jazz Festival, during a celebration of his seventieth birthday, again sans trumpet, to thunderous applause.

Doc, you don't understand. My whole life, my whole soul, my whole spirit is to blow that horn.

—*Louis Armstrong*

Reinvigorated, he began playing trumpet again, against doctor's advice, and in September played a two-week gig with the All-Stars in Las Vegas.[77] In October he returned to England and by year's end made appearances on several television shows: *The Tonight Show Starring Johnny Carson*, *The Flip Wilson Show*, *The David Frost Show*, and *The Johnny Cash Show*. In February of 1971, he performed "Pennies from Heaven" with Bing Crosby in yet another television appearance.

Later that year Louis suffered another heart attack and was again hospitalized. Returning home, he created two new collages, the front and back of a single tape box, out of newspaper headlines outlining his recovery, ". . . heaven will have to wait for ol' Louis." He called his manager that evening and told him he was ready to play, to get the boys back together. He died in his sleep the following morning, July 6, 1971.

"He left an undying testimony to the human condition in the America of his time."—*Wynton Marsalis*

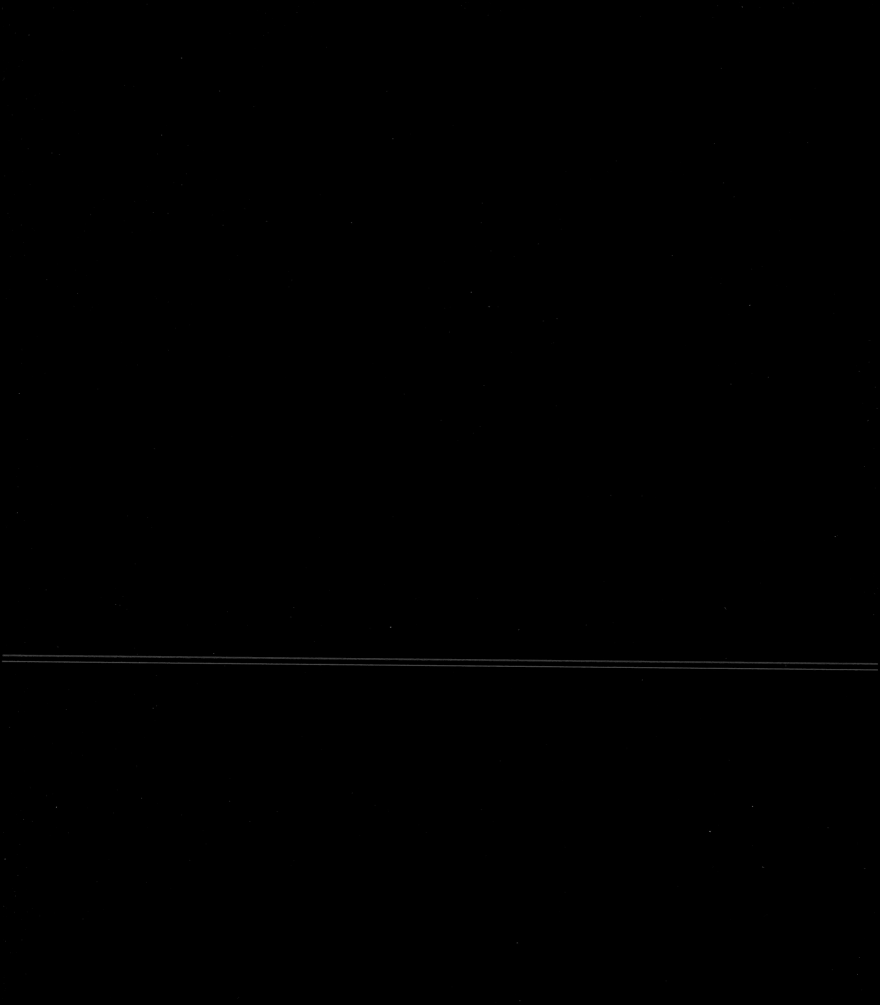

I Hope Gabriel Likes My Music

Twenty-five thousand mourners filed past his casket, as Louis lay in wait at the Seventh Regiment Armory in Manhattan. The honorary pallbearers included: Pearl Bailey, Count Basie, Johnny Carson, Dick Cavett, Bing Crosby, Duke Ellington, Ella Fitzgerald, David Frost, Dizzy Gillespie, Merv Griffin, Bobby Hackett, Harry James, Alan King, Mayor John Lindsay, Guy Lombardo, Governor Nelson Rockefeller, Frank Sinatra, Ed Sullivan, and Earl Wilson.

The funeral was held on July 9, at the Corona Congregational Church. Lucille insisted that no service be held until Lil Hardin could arrive.[78] Lucille received twenty thousand letters of condolence. One was simply addressed to "Mrs. Satchmo, Queens, New York, America," and was delivered.

President Nixon issued a statement:

Mrs. Nixon and I share the sorrow of millions of Americans at the death of Louis Armstrong. One of the architects of an American art form, a free and individual spirit, and an artist of worldwide fame, his great talents and magnificent spirit added richness and pleasure to all our lives.

Many others paid tribute in the lengthy obituary in *The New York Times*:

If anybody was Mr. Jazz it was Louis Armstrong. He was the epitome of jazz and always will be. He is what I call an American standard, an American original. —*Duke Ellington*

We were almost like brothers. I'm so heartbroken over this. The world has lost a champion. —*Earl Hines*

The U.S. State Department issued the following:

His memory will be enshrined in the archives of effective international communications. The Department of State, for which he traveled on tours to almost every corner of the globe, mourns the passing of this great American.

Satchmo, as the world affectionately knew him, who started in this world as Louis Daniel Armstrong, on August 4, 1901, was laid to rest in Flushing Cemetery with an inscription that reads:

LOUIS SATCHMO ARMSTRONG
JULY 4, 1900
JULY 6, 1971

Musicians where I come from, they don't retire, they just stop playing more gigs. —*Louis Armstrong*

Following his passing, Intermediate School 227, close to his home in Corona, was renamed the Louis Armstrong Middle School.

A ten-foot-high bronze statue of Louis, by Elizabeth Catlett, was erected at the center of Louis Armstrong Park in New Orleans. It was originally begun in 1970 and financed by Bing Crosby and other Hollywood entertainers.

By the end of his life, Louis had lost track of the number of recordings he made, but it has been estimated that there are as many as fifteen hundred. He was posthumously awarded the Grammy Lifetime Achievement Award in 1972.

On July 4, 1973, Mayor Lindsay renamed Singer Bowl in Queens the Louis Armstrong Memorial Stadium.

Pan Am World Airways, for the second time in history, honored an individual by naming one of its planes, a Boeing 707, "The Clipper Satchmo" in honor of Louis. The only other person so honored was Copernicus, the great astronomer of the Middle Ages.

In 1991 it was announced by Paris officials that Armstrong, along with artists Marc Chagall and Joan Miró, would have, respectively, an intersection, a street, and a small park named for them, appropriately in the working class 13th Arrondissement. Louis once again confounded the concept of "high" and "low" art.

When I see people smiling, tapping their feet and having a good time I think I must be doing something right. —*Louis Armstrong*

In 1999, President Clinton announced that Armstrong's trumpet was among several items of national memorabilia that were to be interred in our National Millennial Time Capsule to be opened in 2099.

Louis Armstrong has a star on the Hollywood Walk of Fame on 7601 Hollywood Boulevard.

On August 4, 2001, the centennial of his actual birth, New Orleans' airport was renamed the Louis Armstrong New Orleans International Airport. Louis's image appears today on statuettes, coffee mugs, dress-up dolls, liquor decanters, even ceramic hash pipes.

His music is heard today in television commercials, movie sound tracks, and Olympic skating routines. In 1987, as part of the sound track for *Good Morning, Vietnam* Louis scored another top of the chart hit with the re-release of "What a Wonderful World."

"Melancholy Blues," recorded by Louis Armstrong and his Hot Seven on May 11, 1927, in Chicago, Illinois, was included on the Voyager Golden Record sent into outer space to represent "one of the greatest achievements of humanity." Across time and space, if there is anyone out there, they get to dig the genius of Pops, Ol' Dippermouth, Little Louis, Satchmo, along with the rest of us.

You just put a little grease on that Cadillac and it will run another 500 miles. —*Louis Armstrong*

"He was born poor, died rich, and never hurt anyone along the way."—*Duke Ellington*

Endnotes

1. Alfred Appel, Jr., *Jazz Modernism: From Ellington and Armstrong to Matisse and Joyce*, New Haven, Yale University Press, 2004, p. 46.
2. *Gary Giddens, Satchmo: The Genius of Louis Armstrong*, New York, Da Capo Press, 2001, p. xii.
3. Bankhead, Tallulah, *"Stachmo and Tullah," Flair*, 1950.
4. Marc H. Miller, ed., *Louis Armstrong: A Cultural Legacy*, University of Washington Press, Queens Museum of Art, 1993, p. 36.
5. Ibid. pp. 22–23.
6. Ibid. p. 48.
7. Thomas Brothers, *Louis Armstrong's New Orleans*, New York, W.W. Norton, 2006, pp. 160–161.
8. Ibid. p. 79.
9. *Bankhead, Flair*, 1950.
10. Gary Giddens, *Louis Armtrong: Satchmo*, (Sony Music) 2000.
11. *Louis Armstrong's New Orleans*, Brothers, p. 48.
12. *The New York Times*, July 7, 1971.
13. Brothers, *Louis Armstrong's New Orleans*, p. 98.
14. Ibid. p. 46.
15. Laurence Bergreen, *Louis Armstrong: An Extravagant Life*, New York, Broadway Books, 1997, p. 148.
16. Brothers, *Louis Armstrong's New Orleans*, p. 71.
17. Appel, *Jazz Modernism*, p. 203.
18. Ibid. p. 8.
19. Bergreen, *Louis Armstrong: An Extravagant Life*, p. 267.
20. Appel, *Jazz Modernism*, p. 41.
21. Bergreen, *Louis Armstrong*, p. 247.
22. Appel, *Jazz Modernism*, p. 30.
23. Brothers, *Louis Armstrong's New Orleans*, p. 231.
24. Giddins, *Satchmo: The Genius of Louis Armstrong*, p. xvi.
25. Michael Cogswell, *Louis Armstrong: The Offstage Story of Satchmo*, Collector's Press Inc, Portland, Oregon, 2003, p. 10.
26. Thomas Brothers, *Louis Armstrong: In His Own Words*, New York, Oxford University Press, 1999, p. 279.
27. Ibid. p. ix.
28. Bergreen, *Louis Armstrong: An Extravagant Life*, p. 246.
29. Giddins, *Satchmo: The Genius of Louis Armstrong*, p. 54.
30. Appel, *Jazz Modernism: From Ellington and Armstrong to Matisse and Joyce*, p. 146.
31. Brothers, *Louis Armstrong's New Orleans*, p. 232.
32. Appel, *Jazz Modernism*, p. 132.
33. Miller, ed., *Louis Armstrong: A Cultural Legacy*, p. 81.
34. Giddins, *Satchmo: The Genius of Louis Armstrong*, p. 61.
35. Bergreen, *Louis Armstrong*, pp. 226–330.
36. Brothers, *Louis Armstrong's New Orleans*, p. 75.
37. Miller, ed. *Louis Armstrong: A Cultural Legacy*, p. 187.
38. Giddins, *Satchmo: The Genius of Louis Armstrong*, p. 90.
39. Appel, *Jazz Modernism*, p. 31.
40. Leslie E. Cabarga, *The Fleischer Story: The Max Fleischer Cartoon Studio in The Golden Age of Animation*, New York, Da Capo Press, 1988.
41. Bergreen, *Louis Armstrong: : An Extravagant Life* p. 362.
42. Craig Bushey, *The Musical Career of Louis Armstrong Before World War II*, 2006.
43. Bergreen, *Louis Armstrong: An Extravagant Life*, p. 265.
44. Ibid. p. 379.
45. Bushey, *The Musical Career of Louis Armstrong Before World War II*, 2006.
46. Appel, *Jazz Modernism*, p. 41.
47. Bergreen, *Louis Armstrong: An Extravagant Life*, p. 384.
48. Ibid, p. 384.
49. Frank Brady, Citizen Welles: *A Biography of Orson Welles*, New York, Charles Scribner's Sons, 1989, p. 333.
50. *New Orleans* DVD, Bret Wood, Kino Video, 2000.
51. Conversation with Michael Cogswell, 2007.
52. Brothers, *Louis Armstrong's New Orleans*, p. 235.
53. Bergreen, *Louis Armstrong:: An Extravagant Life*, p. 439.
54. Nat Hentoff, *When I Pick Up That Horn, That's All: The life and music of Louis Armstrong*.
55. Brothers, *Louis Armstrong's New Orleans*, p. 81.
56. Bergreen, *Louis Armstrong: An Extravagant Life*, p. 444.
57. *Hugues Panassié, Louis Armstrong*, New York, Da Capo Press, 1971, p. 22.
58. Brothers, *Louis Armstrong's New Orleans*, p. 160.
59. Ibid. p. 161.
60. Cogswell, *Louis Armstrong: The Offstage Story of Satchmo*, p. 33.
61. Krin Gabbard, *Review*, SUNY at Stony Brook.

62. Miller, ed., *Louis Armstrong: A Cultural Legacy*, p. 209.

63. Ibid. p. 213.

64. Thomas Brothers and others apply these terms to jazz, and Louis's playing, but the same holds true for his approach to collage.

65. Bergreen, *Louis Armstrong: An Extravagant Life*, p. 460.

66. Scott Yanow, All Music Guide.

67. Panassié, *Louis Armstrong*, p. 22.

68. *The New York Times*, July 7, 1971.

69. Bergreen, *Louis Armstrong: An Extravagant Life*, p. 470.

70. Ibid. p. 395.

71. Ibid. p. 486.

72. *The New York Times*, Sunday, Sept. 23, 2007.

73. Bergreen, *Louis Armstrong: An Extravagant Life*, p. 471

74. Giddins, *Satchmo: The Genius of Louis Armstrong* , p. 26

75. Leonard Feather, *The Real Louis Armstrong, Down Beat*, March 1, 1962.

76. Bergreen, *Louis Armstrong: An Extravagant Life*, p. 490.

77. Ibid. pp. 490–492.

78. Cogswell, *Louis Armstrong: The Offstage Story of Satchmo*, p. 141.

Bibliography

Appel, Jr., Alfred. *Jazz Modernism: From Ellington and Armstrong to Matisse and Joyce*. New Haven: Yale University Press, 2004.

Armstrong, Louis, *Satchmo: My Life in New Orleans*, Centennial Edition, Introduction by Dan Morgenstern, 1986, New York: Da Capo Press, 2000.

Bankhead, Tallulah. *Flair, Satchmo and Talluh*, 1950.

Bergreen, Laurence. *Louis Armstrong: An Extravagant Life*. New York: Broadway Books, 1997.

Brady, Frank. *Citizen Welles: A Biography of Orson Welles*. New York: Charles Scribner's Sons, 1989.

Brothers, Thomas. *In His Own Words*. New York: Oxford University Press, 1999.

———. *Louis Armstrong's New Orleans*. New York: W.W. Norton, 2006.

Bushey, Craig, The Musical Career of Louis Armstrong Before World War II, 2006.

Cabarga, Leslie E. *The Fleischer Story: The Max Fleischer Cartoon Studio in the Golden Age of Animation*. New York: Da Capo Press, 1988.

Chilton, John. *Who's Who of Jazz*. Time-Life Records Special Edition, 1978.

Cogswell, Michael, *Louis Armstrong: The Offstage Story of Satchmo*, Portland, Oregon: Collector's Press Inc., 2003.

Crumb, Robert. *Heroes of Blues, Jazz & Country*. New York: H. N. Abrams, 2006.

Feather, Leonard. *The Real Louis Armstrong. Down Beat*, March 1, 1962.

Gabbard, Krin. *Review*, SUNY at Stony Brook.

Giddins, Gary. *Satchmo: The Genius of Louis Armstrong*. New York: Da Capo Press, 2001.

Hentoff, Nat. *When I Pick Up That Horn, That's All: The Life and Music of Louis Armstrong. Gadfly*, March/April 2000. http//www.gadflyonline.com/archive/MarchApril00

Jones, Max, and John Chilton. *Louis: The Long Armstrong Story*. Boston, Toronto: Little, Brown and Company, 1971.

Louis Armstrong: A Cultural Legacy, edited by Marc H. Miller. University of Washington Press, Queens Museum of Art, 1993.

Louis Armstrong: Satchmo, DVD. Directed by Gary Giddins. Sony Music, 2000.

Margolick, David. "The Day Louis Armstrong Made Noise," *The New York Times*, Sunday, September 23, 2007.

Meggs, Philip B., and Alston W. Purvi. *Meggs' History of Graphic Design*, 4th ed., New York: Wiley, 2005.

http://www.michaelminn.net/armstrong/index.php

Panassié, Hugues. *Louis Armstrong*, New York: Da Capo Press, 1971.

Pasquet, *Louis Armstrong*. Antwerpen, Belgium: Bries, 2001.

http://www poemhunter.com/lyrics/louis-armstrong/biography

http://www redhotjazz.com/lao.html

http://www satchmo.net

http://www swingmusic.net/ArmstrongLouis.html

Wescher, Herta, *Collage*, Harry N. Abrams, New York, 1968.

Wood, Bret, *The Story of Jazz Essay*, New Orleans DVD, Kino Video, 2000.

Yanow, Scott, All Music Guide. http://www.scottyanow.com

A Louis Armstrong Glossary

The following are terms that Louis is either credited with creating or introduced into the American lexicon:

Cats: Form of address, a musician who plays jazz, someone who digs jazz. "Cat? A cat can be anybody from the guy in the gutter to a lawyer, doctor, the biggest man and the lowest man, but if he's in there with a good heart and enjoyin' the same music together, he's a cat."—Louis Armstrong

Chops: Skill a musician possesses in playing an instrument

Crazy: Good, wonderful

Daddy: Form of address

Dig: Appreciate

Dig them: To understand

Face: Form of address

Gage: Marijuana

Gasser: Sensational

Gate: Form of address for a male, based on one of Louis' early nicknames, Gatemouth

Groovy: To be in the groove, fine

Gutbucket: To play lowdown, playing your heart out, after the pail that caught the innards of cleaned fish; one of the many terms Louis applied to the form of music he played, which later came to be known by white audiences as "jazz"

Homes: A guy from the neighborhood, or hometown

Jive: jazz or swing music, a very lively, uninhibited style of popular dancing, the slang used by jazz musicians, smooth talk that is often deceptive or insincere

Latch on: To understand, grab, take hold

Mellow: Good, cool, fine

Muggles: Marijuana

Pops: Affectionate form of address for males

Savvy: Do you understand?

Scat: To improvise nonsensical lyrics

Send: To arouse the emotions

Sender: A musician

Solid: Approval, consent, or appreciation

Swing it, Gate: To play enthusiastically

Terrible: Approval, consent, or appreciation

Vipers: Marijuana smokers

You cats: Band members

Editor: Eva Prinz
Designer: Steven Brower
Production Manager: Anet Sirna-Bruder

Library of Congress Cataloging-in-Publication Data

Brower, Steven, 1969-
Satchmo : the wonderful world and art of Louis Armstrong / by
Steven Brower ;
introduction by Hilton Als.
    p. cm.
ISBN 978-0-8109-9528-4
1. Armstrong, Louis, 1901-1971. 2. Jazz musicians—United
States—Biography. I. Title.

ML419.A75B83 2009
781.65092—dc22
  [B]

                    2008031632

Printed and bound in China
10 9 8 7 6 5 4 3 2 1

Abrams books are available at special discounts when purchased in
quantity for premiums and promotions as well as fundraising or educational use. Special editions can also be created to specification. For
details, contact specialmarkets@hnabooks.com or the address below.

HNA ▌▌▌▌▌
harry n. abrams, inc.
a subsidiary of La Martinière Groupe
115 West 18th Street
New York, NY 10011
www.hnabooks.com

This book was set in Gil Sans, designed by Eric Gil in 1927–1930.
The paper was manufactured in South Korea, the endpapers in
Indonesia, and it was printed and bound in China.

Acknowledgments

I have been truly blessed to be surrounded by folks whose generosity
rivaled Louis's own throughout his life. Thank you all. First and foremost,
to Eva Prinz, my editor, muse, and guide, whose unflagging support,
loyalty, and creativity has meant more to me than I could ever express.
To her friend the artist Tom Sachs, for first telling us about the collages.
To Phoebe Jacobs of the Louis Armstrong Foundation, who championed
this book from the beginning, graciously shared her recollections and
love of Louis, and made it happen. At the Louis Armstrong Archive, I
cannot thank Michael Cogswell enough for his willingness to share his
extensive knowledge and enthusiasm; likewise, Baltsar Beckeld and
Lesley Zlabinger for all their hard work. At Harry N. Abrams, Eric
Himmel, Editor in Chief, for all his unwavering support and clear-eyed
guidance; to art director Michelle Ishay, who dug Satchmo from the
very beginning, and her assistant Kara Strubel; to Eva's assistant Sofia
Gutiérrez; and to Anet Sirna-Bruder and Alison Gervais in the production
department for bringing this book into reality. To Oscar Cohen of the
Associate Booking Corporation, and Dan Morgenstern and Tad Hershorn
at the Institute for Jazz Studies at Rutgers University. To Hilton Als for
his wonderful foreword and Thurston Moore for making it happen. To
my online friends Stan Taylor and Glen Story for sharing and their
insight, to life-long friends Norris Burroughs and Philip Milito for the
same, and lastly, to Kati and Janna, for continuing to put up with me.